Cults AND CHRISTIAN Counterfeits

Cults AND CHRISTIAN Counterfeits

BRUCE D. WOODS

MOUNTAIN ARBOR PRESS
Alpharetta, GA

The opinions expressed in this book are those of the author and are based upon information and data obtained by the author at the time of publication.

Copyright © 2022 by Bruce D. Woods

All rights reserved. No part of this book may be reproduced or transmitted in any form or by any means, electronic or mechanical, including photocopying, recording, or any information storage and retrieval system, without permission in writing from the author.

ISBN: 978-1-6653-0381-1 - Paperback
eISBN: 978-1-6653-0382-8 - eBook

These ISBNs are the property of Mountain Arbor Press for the express purpose of sales and distribution of this title. The content of this book is the property of the copyright holder only. Mountain Arbor Press does not hold any ownership of the content of this book and is not liable in any way for the materials contained within. The views and opinions expressed in this book are the property of the Author/Copyright holder, and do not necessarily reflect those of Mountain Arbor Press.

∞This paper meets the requirements of ANSI/NISO Z39.48-1992 (Permanence of Paper)

Scripture quotations marked "KJV" are taken from the Holy Bible, King James Version (Public Domain).

Scripture quotations marked "NKJV" are taken from the New King James Version®. Copyright © 1982 by Thomas Nelson. Used by permission. All rights reserved.

042822

*In loving memory of Helen Soderstrum.
She opened the Bible for me and changed my life.*

CONTENTS

Author's Note   ix
Introduction   xi
   – *Definitions*
   – *Fundamental Christian Beliefs*

CHAPTER 1   Major Heresies   1

CHAPTER 2   Twenty Ways Cults Misread the Bible   9

CHAPTER 3   Why Cults Became Popular   29

CHAPTER 4   Seven Warning Sings   33

CHAPTER 5   Some False Teachings   35
   – The Prosperity Gospel
   – Deism
   – Legalism and Antinomianism

CHAPTER 6   Some Western Cults   43
   – Jehovah's Witnesses
   – Christian Science
   – Mormons/Church of Jesus Christ LDS
   – Unitarian/Universalist
   – Scientology
   – Unification Church
   – New Age

CHAPTER 7 Two Groups in Transition   57
  – Grace Communion International (formerly Worldwide Church of God)
  – Seventh-Day Adventists

CHAPTER 8 Some Eastern Cults   61
  – Zen Buddhism
  – Bahá'í
  – Hare Krishna (ISKCON/TM)

CHAPTER 9 Some Occult Groups   67
  – Kabbalah
  – Astrology
  – Satanism
  – Witchcraft/Wicca
  – Rosicrucianism
  – Spiritism
  – Theosophy

CHAPTER 10 Some Facts about Islam   75

CHAPTER 11 Christianity and Secret Societies   77

Conclusion   79
  – *Dos and Don'ts*
  – *What We Can Learn From Cults*
  – *Snapshot Evalutation of Some Cult Beliefs*

Appendix A   81
Appendix B   83
Appendix C   85
Appendix D   89
Acknowledgments   95
Bibliography   97

AUTHOR'S NOTE

There is a wonderful teaching in Luke 10:25–28 (NKJV), which is often overlooked when reading the story, where Jesus related about the Good Samaritan. A lawyer asks Jesus a profound question: "Teacher, what shall I do to inherit eternal life?" Jesus responds by asking the lawyer two questions in return: "What is written in the Law? What is your reading of it?" The lawyer quotes Deuteronomy 6:5 and Leviticus 19:18 by saying, "You shall love the Lord your God with all your heart, with all your soul, with all your strength, and with all your mind, and your neighbor as yourself" (NKJV).

Jesus acknowledged that the lawyer had answered correctly and told him "to go and do likewise." But the lawyer was an intelligent man and quickly discerned he could not live up to these commands of God. No one can do that.

But that's what God demands of those who wish to be with Him in heaven. Since no person can fully live up to God's demands of us, we need help in a big way. We—every one of us on the planet—need a savior. Jesus became a man so that His death would include taking on the sins of all. God required payment for all of mankind's sin-debt and only Jesus's perfect life, perfect obedience, and substitutionary atonement were sufficient.

The question the lawyer asked is probably the most important question you could ever ask, and, regardless of what you believe, you need the real answer to this important question. You need to accept the magnificent gift of God's grace through Jesus Christ. It is eternally valuable and costs nothing.

I have compiled this short—hopefully readable—book to present the basics of Christianity and how several of the "other" counterfeit solutions fail to address the real problems and issues of life. Any factual errors or typos are 100 percent my fault. I'll ask you to read past my clumsy prose and see the eternal light that only Jesus can offer.

—Bruce D. Woods

INTRODUCTION

This is not a book that attempts to judge people or their beliefs. The attempt here is to outline the fundamental beliefs of Christianity and those of some other belief systems. Just as all those who profess to be Christians are not necessarily Christians, all those who follow or belong to other groups are not automatically non-Christians. Judgments of the heart and soul are reserved for God alone. However, if you are a follower of Christ and/or members of His church, you should learn as much as you can about your own faith to better prepare you for the constant barrage of secular and anti-Christian messages offered by the ill-informed, or as an orchestrated part of Satan's ongoing effort to destroy God's children. There's a line from an old movie I like, "If you're not committed, you're just taking up space." Christians have to be committed and at least as informed and strong in their faith as those who try to sell other belief systems and philosophies which often are truly anti-Christian in nature.

Definitions

The following definitions are *not* secular or unbiased. You will see other definitions in a typical dictionary. These definitions assume a Christian point of view. The use of a word like *cult* is not meant to be derogatory. It is used to clearly classify a belief system that is grossly at odds with orthodox Christianity. Mainstream media *could* label, for example,

Presbyterianism a cult per an agnostic or secular viewpoint or deem Christian Science a Christian group. This book uses Christianity as its frame of reference and comparisons—a faith based upon the single source we call the Holy Bible.

Apostasy [apostate belief systems]: Renunciation of Jesus Christ as the Son of God and His being one with the Father—more generally the renunciation of the Church. The broader definition of apostasy for Christians includes all religions and faith systems that are clearly not Christian in most aspects. These religions do not pretend to be partly Christian, another branch of Christianity, or a "new revelation" of Christianity. Apostate systems include all the other major world religions—Buddhism, Hinduism, Confucianism, Islam, Shintoism, etc.

Cult: From a Christian perspective, a cult is a set of beliefs and practices which are significantly at odds with orthodox Christianity. From a Christian standpoint, these beliefs are considered heretical. Many cults are based on significantly distorted definitions of Christian terms and/or distorted or grossly inaccurate interpretations (or false "translations") of the Scriptures. Most cults deny or diminish the deity of Christ.

Heresy: A religious opinion significantly at odds with church dogma and generally accepted Christian beliefs. Many heresies attack the deity of Christ. Others attempt to add to or detract from the Bible with "new" revelations and theories about the foundations of Christianity. Still, others play to the naïve, with calls for "unity" or "let's find a common ground" or even "compromise so that others might not be offended." The Bible doesn't need to be reinterpreted per the current culture! The words of Jesus are often gentle and always wise but they are not ambivalent nor are they to be taken lightly.

Occult: These belief systems are based on "knowledge" beyond the bounds of the rational mind. Occult beliefs are often based on secret revelations to one or just a few others and are not independently verifiable. Occult groups often ask their followers to accept behavior and practices which are deviant or illegal, including drug use, sensory deprivation, and sexual practices involving minors or degrading women. Some of these groups—like noxious weeds resistant to a weed killer—have been around in some form or another for thousands of years.

Sect: A sect, from a Christian viewpoint, is a Christian group that is not considered a "mainline" denomination and may have one or more practices that separate them from most Christian churches. A sect (per this definition) accepts the deity of Jesus and most Christian core beliefs. Examples include the Old Order Amish and the Salvation Army.

Fundamental Christian Beliefs

This list of attributes that attend Christianity across virtually all denominations and major branches of Christendom can be categorized using several means. The following fifteen basic tenets of Christianity is one that I chose. Others who have defined Christianity have used fewer but broader fundamentals for Christianity. I chose a longer list because there are some cult systems that would claim they are "in agreement" with the major tenets of Christianity but, in actuality, when you delve into the details of what they believe, you often find deviant, unbiblical beliefs that orthodox Christianity does not share. A non-exhaustive list of Bible passages that support these beliefs is noted with each. Appendix B compares the seven groups labeled "cults" with the fifteen basic tenets described below.

One: The Bible is the only written Word of God. It is fully trustworthy, authoritative, and is a completed work. It is the basis of the Christian faith.
Bible Passages: Deut. 4:2, 12:32; Prov. 30:5–6; Gal. 1:8; 2 Tim. 3:16–17; Heb. 1:1-2; 1 John 5:13; Rev. 22:18–19.

Two: God exists and is revealed in three persons—Father, Son, and Holy Spirit.
Bible Passages: Matt. 3:13–17, 28:19; John 6:27, 10:30, 14:9; Acts 5:3–9; 2 Cor. 13:14; Col. 2:9.

Three: Jesus Christ became a man at the incarnation and has always been truly God, a person of the Trinity.
Bible Passages: Matt. 11:27, 14:33; Mark 10:45; John 1:1, 1:13–14, 8:42, 10:30, 10:36, 14:6; 1 Cor. 8:6; Col. 1:17; Heb. 4:14–15; 1 John 4:15; Rev. 22:13–17.

Four: The Holy Spirit is truly God.
Bible Passages: Job 33:4; Ps. 104:30; Matt. 28:19; Mark 3:29, 12:36, 13:11; Luke 1:15, 4:1, 12:12; John 14:26, 20:22; Acts 5:3–4, 8:29; 1 Cor. 2:10, 3:16–17, 12:11–12; 2 Cor. 13:14.

Five: Man is sinful by nature.
Bible Passages: Jer. 17:9; Rom. 1:18, 3:23, 5:12; Eph. 2:1; 1 John 1:8.

Six: Satan is a fallen angel and tempts people to turn from God.
Bible Passages: Gen. 3; Matt. 4:1–11; Luke 10:18; 2 Cor. 12:7.

Seven: Jesus was conceived by the Holy Spirit.
Bible Passages: Matt. 1:18, 20; Luke 1:35.

Eight: Jesus was born of a virgin.
>**Bible Passages:** Gen. 3:15; Isa. 7:14; Matt. 1:23; Luke 1:26–34.

Nine: Jesus died and was raised bodily from the dead.
>**Bible Passages:** Matt. 28:1–10; Mark 16:1–8; Luke 24:1–43; John 20, 21; 1 Cor. 2:2, 15:3–6.

Ten: Jesus ascended bodily to Heaven.
>**Bible Passages:** Luke 24:51; John 16:7; Acts 1:9–10, 2:33; Rom. 8:34; Eph. 4:8; 1 Pet. 3:22.

Eleven: Jesus has fully atoned for the sins of mankind.
>**Bible Passages:** John 3:16, 5:24; Acts 2:21; Rom. 5:18, 10:13; 1 Cor. 5:7; Heb. 9:26–28; 1 Pet. 3:18.

Twelve: Faith in Jesus Christ alone saves us from the eternal consequences of sin.
>**Bible Passages:** John 4:25–26; Acts 4:12; Rom. 3:24, 5:1, 10:9–10; 1 Cor. 15:3; Eph 2:8–9; Phil. 2:10–11; Titus 3:5–7.

Thirteen: Jesus will return to judge mankind.
>**Bible Passages:** Zech. 12:9–11; Matt. 24:30; 1 Thes. 4:16–17; Rev. 1:7.

Fourteen: Heaven is the eternal reward for the saved.
>**Bible Passages:** Ps. 16:11; Isa. 49:10; Dan. 12:1–3; Matt. 5:12, 13:43; Luke 12:37; John 12:26, 14:1–4, 17:24; 1 Cor. 2:9; 1 Pet. 1:4; Rev. 7:16, 14:13, 21:4, 22:3.

Fifteen: Hell is the punishment for the lost.
Bible Passages: Ps. 9:17; Prov. 5:5, 7:27, 9:18; Matt. 5:22, 8:11–12, 13:42, 50, 22:13; Luke 13:24–28; 2 Pet. 2:4, 17; Jude 13; Rev. 14:9–11.

CHAPTER 1

Major Heresies

The following list (in alphabetical order) is not an exhaustive list of heresies, per the viewpoint of orthodox Christianity, but it does briefly describe some of them, including the more pervasive ones. (Consult Harold O. J. Brown's book in the bibliography for much more detail about heresies, how they got started, and how they changed over time.)

Apollinarianism: Named after Apollinarius, bishop of Antioch, this theory held that Christ had no human soul or spirit—only a divine one. Apollinarius reasoned that because Jesus was free of sin, He was purely divine. If Christ was not fully human, then His suffering was meaningless. Only if Christ was fully human could He have suffered temptation, hunger, thirst, pain, and death. Subtle forms of this heresy persist today.

Arianism: This idea was popularized by Arius, an Alexandrian priest. It started as a reaction to what Arius called the "Sabellianism of his bishop"—a.k.a. Modalistic Monarchianism. Though it is true that nowhere in the

Bible is Jesus Christ called "the eternal Son of God," and He is never called Son until the incarnation—except in prophecies of Him and His coming in the Old Testament—it is *not* true that the second person of the Trinity was created by God or has not been an eternal person of the triune God.

John's gospel makes it clear that, before the incarnation, Jesus was the eternal Logos—the Word of God. Jesus was always part of the Trinity and was not a created being, regardless of whether you view Him as the Logos or the Son of God before the incarnation. Arius's gross misunderstanding of the second person of the Trinity is completely at odds with a fundamental tenet of Christianity. A strong rebuttal of this heresy was voiced at the Council of Nicaea and is summarized in the Nicene Creed. Several cults have embraced this heresy as part of their belief systems.

Docetism: The name is derived from the Greek word *dokesis* meaning "to seem." This heresy claims that Jesus Christ was not a real human being—He only seemed to be a man and did not have a real human body. This was yet another attack against the claim that Jesus was both fully human and fully divine—a foundational doctrine of Christianity.

Gnosticism: The Gnostics were a sect older than Christianity itself. They initially started with a Jewish faith but over time they mixed in many eastern myths and Greek philosophy into their belief system (*gnosis* is the Greek word for knowledge.) The Gnostics came to believe that God was good and, therefore, He could not have created the world which contains evil. To explain the creation, they posed that his various "children" created the physical world—à la the Greek system of gods and goddesses. One such child was Jesus who was born to share "secret knowledge" from God (unwritten and passed on verbally). The Gnostics claimed that knowledge to be only a part of their religion.

The Gnostics believed that all matter was evil, including the human body, and that Christ's divine spirit only descended into the man Jesus at His baptism and left Him before His crucifixion, leaving only the human man—and not Christ—to suffer and die on the cross. The Gnostics themselves were not a unified group, and among them were several groups that held various other beliefs along similar lines.

The remnant of Gnosticism that continues to trap the unwary is their belief that Jesus was not fully God nor fully human. For the Gnostics, the secret knowledge was the key to salvation for spirits separate from the evil material world. For Christians, the key to salvation is God's sacrifice of His divine Son. If that sacrifice was not of God Himself, then how could it possibly atone for all of man's sin? The claim that only the man Jesus died versus the foundation of Christianity (Jesus was the Son of God, both fully divine and fully human who was crucified, dead, buried, and raised from the dead) are, of course, completely at odds with each other. One early church response to the "gnostic heresy" was the Apostle's Creed. But the gnostic heresy lives on through several cults.

Monarchianism: This heresy was promulgated primarily through two variants. *Dynamic Monarchianism*—also known as Adoptionism—claimed that Jesus was an ordinary man in whom divine power had been placed by God. This power was conferred to Jesus at His baptism and again after His resurrection. Thus, in this heresy, Jesus was fully man but *not* fully God—only a man who was granted divine power for His ministry before the cross and then before the ascension. *Modalistic Monarchianism*, or Sabellianism, claimed that the Trinity was three different modes, or different aspects, of God. God, they believed, would manifest Himself as the Father, the Son, and the Holy Spirit, whenever He found it necessary. This more subtle variant is probably believed by a significant number of Christians as they fail to grasp that the Godhead is three persons yet fully one God. This heresy suggests that God uses Jesus and the Holy Spirit as different modes to interact with His creation and people. Modalistic Monarchianism denigrates the Person of Christ and the Person of the Holy Spirit when it is quite plain that they have both operated using the plan of God with complete divine authority and not just as modes of God. It fails to explain why Jesus would so often pray to the Father or why the Holy Spirit, though fully divine, was sent by God in the Old Testament and sent by Jesus after His resurrection to be with us now in the New Testament.

The Bible makes it clear that these three are persons of God, not modes of operation. The Trinity concept is the best way that we humans can describe God and His divinity, and despite the fact that it's not an easy concept to grasp, it is not polytheism nor is it three modes of operation.

Monophysitism: This heresy claims that Jesus was God with human attributes. But Jesus's nature as fully man and fully God is denied—a major tenet of Christianity. This belief still exists within some Eastern Christian churches.

Nestorianism: This heresy has been attributed to Nestorius, bishop of Antioch. With a confused sense of logic, this heresy claimed that because Christ was eternally God, He could not have been born of Mary. Therefore, Jesus was host to two separate persons—the Son of God and the son of a mortal man (presumably Joseph?). As stated before, Jesus was, in fact, one person who was fully human and fully divine—a significant and essential difference for Christians.

Pelagianism: Named after Irish monk Pelagius, this heresy claimed that original sin was *not* passed down through humanity from Adam and Eve. Additionally, it claimed that baptism was not considered a means of grace nor was it needed. People could be saved by their own efforts and not necessarily by the grace of God. Some Christians today believe one or more aspects of this heretical viewpoint.

Syncretism: This term covers the broad subject of mingling biblical truths with pagan customs and practices. While not, per se, a heresy, syncretism can well lead to heretical beliefs and practices. This was a significant problem in the early church—especially for converts from pagan cultures, and Paul spent considerable efforts trying to keep pagan practices and beliefs out of Christian worship and teachings. The danger lies in how pagan practices and beliefs are handled. If they become mere times for celebration or are completely sublimated to Christian practices and beliefs, they can be harmless. But if there is any accommodation of pagan practices or beliefs or attempts to legitimize them, then syncretism can be dangerous. Secret societies often have "belief systems" that mix legends, pagan beliefs, heretical beliefs, and parts of Christianity into their rituals, practices, and oaths.

Examples of syncretism in modern-day life include:

- The choice of December 25 for the birth date of Jesus was originally the date to celebrate the birth of the sun god.

- As it happens, the best evidence is that Jesus was born on June 2, 2 BC and the visit of the Magi took place on December 25, 2 BC. So the first celebration of Jesus's birth with gifts may well have taken place on the day that was a pre-Christian birthday for a pagan god!
- Another example is Mardi Gras, a pre-Lenten festival that came from pagan celebrations of the end of winter and the vernal equinox.
- The use of Easter eggs came from the Persian and Egyptian custom of decorating eggs in the spring as symbols of fertility. Rabbits are also pre-Christian symbols of fertility for an obvious reason.
- Valentine's Day comes from a pagan Roman festival under the patronage of Juno, goddess of marriage. Juno was replaced by St. Valentine, patron saint of love.
- Halloween stems from an ancient pagan Celtic festival to ward off ghosts.
  - In the eighth century, the Roman Church decreed November 1 to be All-Saints Day—a day to remember and honor Christians deemed as saints. However, despite the attempt by Christianity to co-opt the festival to ward off ghosts, Halloween now focuses a lot more on ghosts and witches than it does on the saints of the church!

A major issue for Christians today is the pressure to compromise the faith or biblical truths in the spirit of ecumenism, "mixed services," or "community worship." Whenever Christ is denied, denigrated, or some questionable practice or belief is incorporated into worship or practice, a heresy may be introduced—often in a harmless guise—which could lead people astray. Nowhere in the Gospel does Jesus imply that His followers should accommodate other beliefs or practices into their lives. Paul's letters also strongly warn against it.

CHAPTER 2

Twenty Ways Cults Misread the Bible

The Bible is, among other things, a unique book in the history of the human race. No other book lays claim to being *the* revelation(s) of God to mankind. No other book offers the answers to all of the important questions. No other book has stood up to both the test of time and the critical attacks by those who choose not to believe in God and remain unscathed. No other book is as valid and relevant now as it has ever been. No other book is filled with prophecies that have either already been fulfilled with stunning accuracy or are expected to be fulfilled in the future. No other book paints a portrait of a God who has always been actively seeking the redemption and salvation of His children, despite the fact that they are all fallen, corrupt people who have no means to save themselves from their sinful natures. What the Bible means to a believer would take countless volumes to describe in detail. It is truly God's Word that has been revealed to us.

Given the unequaled, incomparable status of the Bible, someone who would offer a fake religion or philosophy might well use the Bible itself to justify aberrant or heretical beliefs. But for the cultist, in-context and accurate renderings of Scripture passages wouldn't help the cause of someone who offers a phony substitute for Christianity. So they use a number of underhanded, sneaky, and often subtle means to undermine what the Scriptures actually say and mean. Twisting the Scriptures in one or more ways is often a means to fool the ignorant or gullible into thinking that the Bible supports the lies and misrepresentations of the cultists. Of course, some cults go beyond misrepresenting what the Bible says by using flawed or invalid "translations," including adding or subtracting to what the Scriptures plainly say. This brief review seeks to highlight the many ways the Bible's meanings and truths are perverted by the enemies of God and Christ.

1. Inaccurate Quotation

This is a particularly effective means if the audience is not familiar with what the Bible actually says. Typically one is confronted by a "quotation from Scripture" taken out of thin air and asked to believe it without verifying it within its context. The main reasons this ploy often is effective are (1) usually the audience is not all that familiar with what the Bible actually says, and (2) people are often cowed into silence or a tacit agreement when the speaker or purveyor of an inaccurate quotation presents it as biblical.

An example of this is the saying "Money is the root of all evil." As misquoted, money itself is inherently evil. But the Bible actually says, in 1 Timothy 6:10 (KJV), "For the love of money is the root of all evil: which while some coveted after, they have erred from the faith, and pierced themselves through with many sorrows." The actual quotation invokes the breaking of two Commandments—making money an idol and coveting after money. It also plainly describes the consequences of those who would idolize and covet money.

Another example is the misquote, "Pride goeth before the fall." The actual passage, from Proverbs 16:18 (KJV), reads, "Pride goeth before destruction and a haughty spirit before a fall." And what is "haughty"? Definitions include arrogance and contemptuous. Surely pride *is* the breeding ground for human sins, and it remains a continuing struggle for a Christian to keep pride's influence at a minimum. But when pride leads one to exhibit arrogance or contempt toward God and His rules, that's a sure recipe for a big fall.

A third example is the misquote "God will not give you more than you can handle." The actual passage, in 1 Corinthians 10:13, reads, "There hath no temptation taken you but such as is common to man: but God is faithful, who will not suffer you to be tempted above that ye are able; but will with the temptation also make a way to escape, that ye may be able to bear it." (I referenced the King James Version here because a misquote is often clothed in King James–style words and usage.) Note the completely different emphasis between the misquote and actual passage—the misquote talks about burdens whereas the actual passage talks about temptation *and* God's promise to limit the temptation and to allow us to escape it.

Misquotes are commonly offered, repeated as if they were accurate passages, and often believed as biblical truth. When someone offers a quote, make sure you know what the biblical reference is; if it is offered without referencing the Bible, be very skeptical of its completeness and truth.

2. Twisted Translation

This can occur in a couple of ways. The first way is through sloppy, inaccurate translations of the best available Hebrew and Greek source materials. I include, as "sloppy, inaccurate" paraphrases, "The Living Bible" and "The Message." Paraphrases are sometimes so aberrant that the original intent of a passage gets completely lost. Paraphrases also tend to be one person's (or a small group's) efforts, which do not get peer reviews, no arguments are heard or weighed about words or phrases or idioms, which may be unclear, and they frequently suffer because they do not get scrutinized by independent editors. Biases, invented doctrines, and mistranslations abound in paraphrases. Much of what is in them was not in the original language sources, and frequently, key original words and ideas are left out.

Under the guises of modernity and readability, paraphrases offer a substandard substitute for real translations. So-called translations to lower the reading level of the Bible or to make the Bible "kid-friendly" also are often deficient in several significant ways.

The other aspect of the twisted-translation error has a more devious motive: purposeful mistranslations to support a notion or doctrine of a cult. I'll offer two examples. The Jehovah's Witnesses' "New World Translation" has a number of purposely mistranslated passages, e.g., John 1:1. The NWT translation reads, "In the beginning, the Word was, and the Word was with God and the Word was a god." The NWT tries to consistently portray Jesus as a created being—not part of the triune God from before time itself. Jehovah's Witnesses have bought into the Arian heresy and do not believe in the Trinity. Other passages that the NWT purposely mistranslates to deny the eternal deity of Christ include Colossians 1:15–17, Philippians 2:6, Titus 2:13, 2 Peter 1:1, Revelation 3:14, and Proverbs 8:22.

The second example of twisted translations is when the Mormons split in the nineteenth century, the majority relocated to Utah; the minority, including Joseph Smith's widow and son, moved to Missouri. The Missouri branch adopted the use of Joseph Smith's "translation," which included many passages that were invented by Smith and are unsupported by any prior source materials. Otherwise, it was a plagiarized King James Version Bible. One invented passage was an added section (verses 24–38) to end Genesis chapter 50 to prophesize Smith's own appearance. Smith's "translation" also added some eighty other passages within the King James Version spread throughout the Old and New Testaments. His zeal to pervert the Bible to his own ends was shameless. When you hear a cult supporter or biblically naïve person quote the Bible, make sure you know what translation is being quoted and its legitimacy. Cults sometimes use their own version of the Bible.

3. The Biblical Hook

Those familiar with fishing know that the best way to land a fish is to get the fish's attention. The attention-getter is often a shiny, flashy lure or one that vibrates or looks like it is swimming. Car dealers know the same set of tricks, and their TV ads often portray attention-getting people to try to get you interested in buying a new car. Note that the pretty girl on TV has almost nothing to do with judging a car on its merits.

So it is with many cult groups: they will trot out a passage of the Bible and then use that to justify or validate what they are doing—often with little or no relationship between the passage and their doctrines or practices. But since the Bible is widely thought to be authoritative and filled with wisdom, cults use the Bible to draw the unsuspecting to them.

The Mormons often use James 1:5—"If any of you lack wisdom, let him ask of God, that giveth to all men liberally, and upbraideth not, and it shall be given him." Using this quote, the Mormons explain that this is exactly what Joseph Smith did—he asked God. And according to Smith, he received a revelation from which he concluded that God the Father has a body. Yet, the passage in James has nothing to do with Smith's conjecture that God has a physical body. Cultists often use "biblical hooks" to attract the unwary.

4. Ignoring the Immediate Context

Alan Watts, a British philosopher who popularized Eastern religions, once quoted John 5:39 as "You search the Scriptures, because you think that in them you have eternal life." He was trying to convey the idea that Jesus was challenging His listeners on the validity of the Old Testament. But the *rest* of verses 39 and 40 read, "and it is they that bear witness to me. Yet you refuse to come to me that you may have life." Obviously, Jesus was upholding the value of the Old Testament as a testimony to Himself.

Another old favorite in this category is "an eye for an eye and a tooth for a tooth"—often quoted as a justification for personal vengeance. The context for this notion is Deuteronomy 19:15–21. Here, God is instructing the civil authorities about witnesses and the need for the rule of law. The emphasis is on meting out deserved punishment in a measured, fair way. This passage has nothing to do with personal vengeance; it is about due process and appropriate punishments for those found guilty. Ignoring the immediate contexts of a passage or picking one short verse from a longer discourse often leads to completely wrong ideas about what the Bible says and means.

5. Collapsing Contexts

This technique has no limits as to how it can be used to justify almost any doctrinal idea that a cult can come up with. For example, the Mormons associate Jeremiah 1:5 with John 1:2 and 14 and conclude that those verses talk about the premortal existence of all human beings—a key Mormon doctrinal belief. However, Jeremiah 1:5 speaks of God's foreknowledge of Jeremiah (not his premortal existence) and John 1:2 refers to the pre-existence of God the Son and not to human beings in general.

6. Overspecification

This is a favorite ploy if you're trying to justify a particular cult doctrine or idea with a Bible verse. Find a verse that *could* possibly be interpreted to support the doctrine in question and interpret it as such and claim that it is a valid interpretation. For example, the Mormon missionary manual quotes the parable of the virgins (Matthew 25:1–13) to document the concept that "mortality is a probationary period during which we prepare to meet God." However, the parable probably does mean something far less specific—human beings should be prepared at any time to encounter God or to witness the Second Coming. There are a lot of other Bible passages that support the concept of being prepared for God or the Second Coming, but I don't know of any Bible passages which reinforce the peculiar Mormon interpretation of this parable.

7. Wordplay

There are some tricks that seem too simplistic to fool anyone but, apparently, even the simple misrepresentations can work. Wordplay is when a word or passage is examined and interpreted as if the revelation was given in that language. For example, Mary Baker Eddy, the grande dame of Christian Science, said the name Adam consists of two syllables—*a dam*, which means an obstruction—in which case, Adam signifies the obstacle which the serpent (sin) would impose between man and his Creator." (Note that it is in English—not Hebrew—that Adam can be curiously mis-thought of as a dam.)

8. The Figurative Fallacy

This can occur when either literal language is mistaken for figurative language *or* when figurative language is mistaken for literal language. Mary Baker Eddy often interpreted the word *evening* in the Bible as "mistiness of moral thought," "weariness of the mortal mind," "obscured views," or "peace and rest." Unless otherwise indicated by its context, the word *evening* in the Bible means evening. If you are willing to ignore the plain, straightforward meanings of the Hebrew and Greek words used to record the Scriptures, you can manipulate the Bible to agree with anything you profess.

The Mormon theologian James Talmage interprets the prophecy that "thou shalt be brought down and speak out of the ground" (from Isaiah 29:4) to mean that God's Word would come to the people from the Book of Mormon which was (supposedly) taken out of the ground at the hill of Cumorah. This mistaken interpretation of figurative language as literal is obviously fallacious if you read the Isaiah passage in its context. The passage in Isaiah is part of a prophecy concerning the city Ariel that has gone seriously astray. Students of the Bible have to guard against assuming what the Bible says agrees with their biases, preconceived notions, and assumptions. It is foolhardy and risky to assume that you alone are capable of discerning and interpreting the Scriptures. Only the Holy Spirit can interpret the Bible. He's available twenty-four seven to help you when you read and study the Bible. He will help you discern what was meant and what it means for you.

9. Speculative Readings of Predictive Prophecy

Another way to twist the Scriptures is to rashly assume that a predictive prophecy is explained or exhibited in current events or events likely to occur soon. Often, the proclaimer of a prophecy coming true has failed to look at the "big picture" across multiple Bible passages or is at odds with many other equally devoted, qualified, biblical scholars. Frequently, the assumption that a biblical prophecy has been (or will soon be) fulfilled is only made by a follower of a particular small segment of a faith—whether it be Christian or a cult.

Two groups pose well as examples: The Jehovah's Witnesses have publicized many elaborate—often specifically dated—prophecies since their beginnings. These prophecies (supposedly found in the Old Testament) gained a lot of attention, as they were to be fulfilled in the near future. They were proven to be mere speculations that may have energized their adherents since none of them came true when they were supposed to. Subsequent pronouncements clarified or recast the prophecies to be fulfilled or even claimed that they came true but in some mysterious way or in secret.

Mormons declare that the "stick of Judah" and the "stick of Joseph," noted in Ezekiel 37:15–22, refer to the Bible and the Book of Mormon. It is obvious from even Ezekiel's florid prose that God is promising a reunification of the Jews within Israel—which has only partly occurred as of yet. Speculative interpretations of prophecy have also caused much damage and proliferation of false doctrines within Christianity, especially the speculations about when Christ will return. Whole sects of Christianity and some cults were formed based on false prophecies and unfounded speculations about the Second Coming. If Jesus Himself says He doesn't know when He will return, why would any human being assume that he might know what Jesus doesn't?

10. Saying But Not Citing

Writers and speakers often use the trick of quoting a passage of the Bible without citing its source. This often indicates that there is no such passage in the Bible. At best, it may mean that the writer or speaker is lazy or sloppy. It also might mean he presumes his audience will believe anything he says without a reference. You've all heard the sayings "God helps those who help themselves," "Cleanliness is next to Godliness," "It is God's desire that you should prosper," "This too will pass," "God moves in mysterious ways," and "All things work together for good." Of course, it's a bit difficult to quote book, chapter, and verse because none of these sayings are in the Bible. Some of the sayings are errant paraphrases of actual Bible verses but they are not even close to what the Bible actually says. Some very wise sayings do come from extra-biblical sources—such as "Hate the sin, love the sinner," which is a loose quote of part of a passage attributed to Mahatma Gandhi. Whenever you hear a saying that is not attributed, remain skeptical about its biblical basis.

11. Selective Citing

If you want to back up your aberrant belief with the Bible, a good method is to pick verses or parts of verses (ignoring their contexts as you will) to support what it postulated. The Jehovah's Witnesses use this technique to support their false belief that Jesus was a created being and is not equal to God in status. The Witnesses claim that Christians mistranslated and misunderstood 1 John 5:7, 1 Timothy 3:16, and John 10:30, further claiming that these passages do not prove the concept of a triune God. This offers them a basis to translate John 1:1, referring to Jesus as "a god"—an obviously errant mistranslation of the Greek text recorded by John. By using selective citing, the Witnesses seek to disprove the Trinitarian nature of God. What the Witnesses do *not* cite are the multiple texts that clearly support the nature of God as a Trinity, including Matthew 28:19; John 20:28; 1 Corinthians 6:11, 12:4–5; 2 Corinthians 1, 21:22, 13:14; Galatians 3:11–14; 1 Thessalonians 5:18–19; 1 Peter 1:1–2. Additionally, Isaiah 6:1, 3, and 10 and John 12:37–41 also testify to the nature of God.

The specious argument that the word *trinity* is not found

in the Bible is a silly one. The word *theocracy* doesn't appear in the Bible either, yet Israel was one for a significant part of its history. It is part of the human struggle to invent words and constructs to help us learn more about God and our relationship with Him. We cannot fully grasp the meaning and the complexity of God the Father, God the Spirit, and God the Son as one inseparable, yet identifiably, different persons within the Godhead. The Trinity concept is the best we have for now. Just because it's hard for us to comprehend God doesn't mean we should fail to try to learn more of Him.

12. Inadequate Evidence

There have been several bizarre attempts to offer alternate theories about how life was formed on Earth. One sci-fi-type theory popularized a few decades ago was that visitors from outer space seeded the earth with plants and maybe animals—as sort of a science experiment? Erich von Daniken speculated about Genesis 6:4 and offered the possibility that Noah's ark was a radio transmitter, referring to Exodus 15:10 and 25:40. He suggested that Sodom and Gomorrah were destroyed by a nuclear explosion, Genesis 19:1–28, and even speculated that Ezekiel saw aliens and a spacecraft in Ezekiel 1:1 and 28. There is *zero* evidence to support these fantasies, either in the Bible or in any other historical account.

But lack of evidence has not deterred the fantasy writers. Another case of inadequate evidence is the Jehovah's Witnesses' claim of a biblical prohibition of blood transfusions. First, God made plain His respect for human life and blood—Genesis 4:8–11 and 9:5–6. Blood is often used to stand for "life" in the Old Testament—see Leviticus 17:11.

God did command His people to not eat blood—Genesis 9:3–4. It is peculiar how a prohibition against eating blood could be taken as a command to abstain from life-giving blood which is transfused. Blood is the essence of life. Jesus shed His blood for us. When someone needs a blood transfusion, why would God forbid an offer to donate blood for someone in need?

Beware: Theories or doctrines based on irrelevant or scant passages of the Bible are likely to be absolutely wrong.

13. Confused Definition

Some confused definitions come from sloppy or errant translations from the original languages. For instance, the commandment which is usually translated "Thou shalt not kill" really was meant to imply "Thou shalt not murder." All taking of human life in all circumstances is not prohibited by God. Self-defense, killings by police or duly authorized civil authorities, and some wars are not prohibited by God. Additionally, God authorized capital punishment for certain types of murder—see Exodus 21:12–17. Imprecise definitions or translations can definitely lead to doctrinal errors.

A more bizarre example was demonstrated when Edgar Cayce (a self-styled prophet) noted that the Sadducees did not believe in the resurrection and then blithely clarified that this meant they didn't believe in reincarnation (which supposedly was what resurrection meant in those days). Sometimes, the Christian concept of being "born again" has also been confused with reincarnation. Some cults embracing reincarnation used the Bible to back up this idea based on a very dubious definition confusion.

14. Ignoring Alternative Explanations

It is a well-known fallacy to adopt a peculiar, fanciful, or eccentric explanation when there is a simple, obvious, and rational explanation. Very rarely does a new or bizarre explanation prove to be correct. The Mormons often use this ploy when trying to sell the Book of Mormon as "divinely inspired." The argument goes like this: After inviting someone to briefly examine the book, they inquire, "As you read each page of the Book of Mormon, pause and ponder. Ask yourself this question again and again: could any *man* have written the book?" The answer the questioner is expecting is "No." The person being asked is likely looking at ornate scripts, chapters, and verses—similar to the Bible. Many people are impressed with the quality of the book and the printing and have no prior knowledge of what the contents actually say or mean. On the spot, the responder may not be thinking clearly and fail to note that the probable answer is that, unless otherwise demonstrated, the book he's reading was written by a human being.

The Bible has a distinct history and influence that no other written volume has ever enjoyed. Though it was recorded by individuals, it clearly was not written from a human standpoint, nor does it reflect multiple, conflicting concepts about God and His creation—despite being recorded over a two thousand years' time frame. The Bible speaks to every culture in any language. All other attempts to emulate the Bible fail because God didn't inspire its creation. The Mormon scriptures don't even agree with each other, let alone the Bible. The Qur'an has been continuously rewritten and re-edited since it first was dubbed as a holy book from Allah. It still is not internally consistent or consistent with the Old Testament that Muslims revere as inspired by God.

15. The Obvious Fallacy

The Jehovah's Witnesses—among others, especially those groups focused on Adventism—often make claims such as "God's Word of truth tells us very clearly that we are fast nearing a worldwide change" (or similar such proclamations). Their supplemental book to the Bible, *The Truth That Leads to Eternal Life*, has such proclamations within it that are to be taken as biblical fact. A Christian response should be something along this line, "No, it doesn't." You can't move easily from scriptural prophecy to a contemporary application. The Scripture does not tell us, very clearly, any such thing. If such a conclusion is actually warranted it would be the result of serious studies of many texts whose particular applications may not be at all clear. (Old adage: a building with no foundation is neither useful nor safe.)

16. Virtue by Association

We know all about "guilt by association," a la "We know that Johnny's been involved in the recent outbreak of shoplifting at the mall because Jimmy was caught stealing there, and Johnny and Jimmy have often played together; they were even on the same Little League baseball team for two years."

The reverse fallacy also is often used. If someone promoting any sort of deviant belief or new twist on Christianity, one of the best ways to promote it is by associating it with some Christian belief, figure, or even a well-regarded Bible passage. Often the promoter of a cult takes great pains to praise Jesus, His teachings, His character, and His works. But in saying so, the next step is often associating another religious figure with Jesus as one who has exhibited the same attributes.

For the Christian, it is well known that Jesus's teachings, character, and works are beyond reproach, but that's not why Jesus is so important. Jesus accomplished a magnificent work that allows any person—whatever their status or circumstances—a way to be cleansed from all unrighteousness, to be forgiven of all sins, and the opportunity to come before God the Father blameless and holy because of what Jesus Christ has done.

There is no other cult, religion, or occult system that can or will make the claim that God Himself removes the stain and guilt of sinfulness and offers that gift to us free and without strings. All other "paths to an eternal life" promoted by the fakes include some sort of variation of self-salvation either by good works or self-improvement via several cycles of living (practice makes perfect?) via reincarnation. Of course, some cults and religions ignore the possibility of life after death, and they limit what their faith system addresses to human life. Virtue by association is an old fallacy but many still fall for it.

Is a product better because some Hollywood star endorses it? Is a variant belief system valid because of some dubious, often irrelevant, comparable traits Jesus and some other leader(s) might share?

The Mormons often use the virtue by association ploy with respect to what they believe to be sacred texts. The Mormons don't deny the Bible; most utilize the King James Bible. But they also claim that three other books are sacred (more on that later when Mormonism is discussed). The typical virtue by association gambit is to get the unwary or naïve to accept the Book of Mormon as also the Word of God by presenting it as the Bible Part II for the Western

Hemisphere. It's organized like the Bible—it has books, chapters, and verses, just like the Bible. In fact, segments of it sound like the Bible because they *are* copied from the King James translation or are obviously altered King James texts. The Mormons put the Bible on a pedestal and then say the other texts deserve similar respect as authoritative revelations from God. Obviously, this fallacy has worked and continues to work in the society at large and in the faith lives of those fooled by the Mormon claims.

17. Esoteric Interpretation

Because the Bible is sometimes difficult to interpret (even by biblical scholars at times), there is always a temptation to assume that the Bible contains a hidden, esoteric meaning which only certain people can uncover.

Who are these special people? Usually, they are leaders of or even founders of cults; sometimes, they write wacko books (filled with sensational revelations) about Bible meanings that were, until now, unknown. Once someone buys into the premise that some gifted guru or mystical scholar has discovered new, previously hidden meanings of scripture, just about anything goes. The self-appointed guru can "discern" anything he wants from a passage, and who's to argue? The naysayer can be dismissed as being unable to grasp the new secret or previously hidden meaning.

The history of cults is filled with such self-appointed interpreters. There are many passages in the Bible that are difficult. Sometimes there are two or three possible meanings based on the best sources. But the biblical scholars argue based on their best understandings and documentation. A postulated view is subject to critiques in the marketplace of ideas. Arguments based on logical fallacies or factual errors are eventually discarded.

But the esoteric guru has no such worries. Their arguments are unverifiable and beyond rational discussions. They may be patently ridiculous but for those who buy into the notion that some special person has insights to the Bible that nobody else can validate, it doesn't matter. Believing in the guru and what they say matters more than believing in God and what His Word actually says. Most cults offer esoteric interpretations of Bible passages to support their beliefs.

18. Supplementing Biblical Authority

Many cults have supplemental books and sources to the Bible (if they use the Bible at all). Mormons have three supplemental books they hold as sacred. The Seventh Day Adventists hold the writings of Ellen White to a level approaching supplemental to the Bible. (I'll say more about that later.) Some Christian churches often overuse secular books in their worship services, education programs, and in study groups. Supplemental sources are like condiments to a fine meal. They can add, amplify, and enhance the experience of the meal. But when the meal becomes eating ketchup, mustard, mayo, ground pepper, and BBQ sauces, you know you've gone way too far. The meat and potatoes of a proper "meal" must be preaching, teaching, and sharing the Gospel and growing one's faith through Bible studies.

19. Rejecting Biblical Authority

It would be nice to believe that cults are the only groups that routinely reject biblical authority. That rejection comes in a few different flavors: certain parts of the Bible are accepted as stated, but other parts are dismissed as legends, myths, allegories, or supplements added later for political or other reasons. The Apocrypha is a group of supplemental books that have been rejected by most Bible scholars. But there are many who do not believe that all sixty-six books considered canonical by Christianity are indeed the Word of God. The cults have long used the "pick and choose" theory about the Bible. However, in the last 150 years or so, influential voices within Christianity itself have also jumped onto the "Reject Biblical Authority" bandwagon. Even mainline Protestant denominations supposedly based on "Scripture alone" have gotten into the act.

The effect of debasing biblical authority as the Word of God and as our rule of faith is like a cancer within the Church. And if cancer is too strong a metaphor for you, then dry rot is certainly an apt description of what rejecting biblical authority will do. Beware of specious, ill-considered arguments that usually are drawn on the artificially contrived Old Testament versus New Testament or law versus grace issues. These arguments are made with the purposeful effect of trying to get the listener to reject part or all of biblical authority.

20. World-View Confusion

This is a nifty trick; it reminds me of watching a magician at work. The world-view confusion works like this. You take a passage from the Bible, strip away how it was contextually relevant and its intentions when it was written, find what agrees with your preconceived notion, and then apply that agreement in a context you decide is relevant.

Of course, the original meaning of that text, within its context and when it was written, is likely to be completely lost or badly distorted after it gets misapplied within a context it was never meant to be part of. It's coincidental that most of this fakery has to do with who Jesus was and what His ministry was all about. The Mormons, Jehovah's Witnesses, and the Unification Church (among several) have used this confusion several times and all have ended up with extraordinarily bizarre doctrines about Jesus and His ministry. If you use fallacious reasoning when reading a Scripture passage, even if your intent is not malicious, you could easily find yourself going down an errant path which could lead to a deviant belief, away from the God you are trying to learn about in the Bible.

CHAPTER 3

Why Cults Became Popular

There have been a number of reasons expressed as to why cults seemed to explode in the 1960s and on. Cults are not a new phenomenon, but the sheer number has grown rapidly in the last half century. Some of the reasons are postulated below:

- **Disillusionment with America (and the world):** The Vietnam War caused a deep rift within the US and was unpopular throughout the world. It seemed as if there was a great concern about Vietnam while the many problems at home were given lower priority. Antiestablishment thinking, which included criticism of churches, became popular.
- **Dehumanization through science and technology:** Computers started controlling our lives—we became numbers. Nuclear war was a real possibility. Those who employed new technologies were considered threats to individual rights and freedoms.

- **The increasing acceptance of the drug culture:** Street drugs have been around for a long time, but they were not acceptable or respectable until the 1960s and later. Relying on drugs to mask the difficulties of life—instead of solving them within a faith construct—seemed easier to do.

- **Fear of the future:** Nuclear bombs, pollution, less-assured job markets, inability to cope with just one wage earner, inflation, gasoline lines, etc.—the optimism of the '50s was replaced with pessimism and doubts.

- **Breakdown of the family:** Wage earners were expected to be mobile. TV became the de facto source for entertainment, news, and values. The increased focus on wealth as a family value contributed to increasing divorce rates.

- **Pop culture:** It was popular to flaunt drug use, and more vulgar language was accepted, creating "alternate" lifestyles and new value systems. It became okay to reject your parent's beliefs.

- **Parapsychology and the occult:** Extrasensory perception (ESP) and hypnosis became favorite media topics. Efforts to legitimatize mysticism were taken up by some respected universities. Phony accounts of supposedly reincarnated pasts recalled through hypnosis were publicized as factual and even scientific accounts.

- **Decline of the church:** Some churches ignored what was happening in the culture. Others responded by neglecting or watering down the Gospel in order to be relevant and fit with current cultural expectations.

Some became dealers in "social gospel" and situation ethics.

- **The ecology crisis:** There was an increasing awareness that pollution and neglect of the environment were harmful and needed to be stopped. The concern about the environment sometimes morphed into beliefs that nature was something to be loved and even worshipped. Some shifted their focus from God to His creation.

- **The rapid increase of the pace of life:** Airplane travel and long-distance calling were now part of everyday culture. People got up earlier and often went to bed later. There were more non-church organizations and activities vying for attention. More time was spent devoted to one's current and next activity away from family activities and discussions. People more often felt like they were alone.

- **Lockdowns and stay-at-home work and schooling:** It's hard to assess the damage COVID-19, and the various edicts and rules enacted to try and halt the spread of this serious virus, has done. Curtailed social lives, community events, church gatherings, and not being with friends and family have markedly changed our social fabric. Barriers to communal worship, school events, and celebrations have been difficult to compensate for. People are social beings and video calls, smartphone messages, and videos are puny substitutes. It's not beyond imagining that there will be more people suffering from depression, anxiety, and the pain that comes from being alone in the near future.

The relative peace and tranquility of the 1950s has been disrupted in many ways. Life has become more chaotic and difficult to deal with. There probably has been a diminished sense of security and purpose. Many have sought security and a renewed sense of purpose. Some found their "answer" in a cult.

CHAPTER 4

Seven Warning Signs

There are several signs that cults or occult groups share that should warn you that they are not based on the divinity of Jesus and, therefore, not part of the Christian church.

1. **Following one human leader:** John the Baptist said of Jesus, "I must decrease, but He must increase." That's the proper pattern: God/Jesus Christ/The Holy Spirit must lead and be the focus of attention. When worship or theology focuses on a human leader, it is improper and can be non-Christian.
2. **Diluting the Bible:** When some person or group adds to the Bible, subtracts from the Bible, or puts other books on a par with the Bible—beware! Another variation is when a group insists that another book or teacher is required to interpret the Bible. The Bible is interpreted through the Holy Spirit only—anyone who reads the Bible has access to the Spirit's power to interpret a passage per God's intent. The Bible *is* the only written Word of God.

3. **Leaving your family:** The family is prominent throughout the Bible. God loves families and it's not His will to break them up so that one member can believe. Leaving one's family is not a prerequisite for belonging to His church or to believe Him.
4. **Forgetting or leaving the church to search for truth:** God gave His truth to the Church. The Church is the body of Christ, and His truth is not revealed within a cult or apostate religion.
5. **Believing "new revelations":** The Bible is a completed document from God to us. It needs no supplements nor is there room for "new revelations."
6. **Avoiding thinking and just believing:** "Believe it because we believe it" is not a good enough reason. God does not lead us contrary to our minds. We don't understand all of God's Word, but we know His Word is not counter to reason or wisdom.
7. **Keeping our secret:** Even the mysteries of the Bible are open for all to read and study. God's truth is not hidden behind a bush waiting for a few clever people to stumble onto and hoard. His Gospel message has not been "lost" or "recently rediscovered." Jesus instructs us to share the Good News, not keep it a secret.

CHAPTER 5

Some False Teachings

The Prosperity Gospel

In a nutshell, the Prosperity Gospel (as it's often referred to) is a false teaching that people who exercise True Faith in Christ will attain physical, material, and financial prosperity in this life.

It began primarily after World War II as a Pentecostal movement. The war was over and jobs with good pay were plentiful. People who underwent rationing were able to buy a new car, a new home, new electrical appliances, and could actually go on nice trips and "see the USA in a Chevrolet." Those whose prosperity was increasing might have thought that the material prosperity was a reward from God—for saving the world from the oppressive Axis regimes.

Even the start of the Cold War with the USSR could not dampen the optimism for the future. Those who were not so blessed to ride the new prosperity of the post-war era were mostly found in the Midwest and South and, if churchgoers, were likely to be worshiping in Baptist or

Pentecostal churches. It was a fertile ground for prosperity gospel teachings.

Oral Roberts, E. W. Kenyon, and Kenneth Hagin led the movement and utilized the power of TV and radio to grow the rolls of those caught up by the message. Later influential leaders of this false gospel included Kenneth Copeland, Creflo Dollar, Benny Hinn, Joel Osteen, T. D. Jakes, John Hagee, Paula White, Joyce Meyer, and Juanita Bynum. These ministers learned well the power of TV and the simplicity of the apparently biblical message. The Trinity Broadcasting Network has been an influential platform for many of these false teachers.

What are the main beliefs?

Jesus purchased all the benefits of salvation for this life. By perverting the teachings of Isaiah 53:5 and John 10:10, the Prosperity Gospel asserts that Jesus died to take away every sickness in this life. Additionally, He will atone for the "sin" of financial poverty. *(Christianity teaches that God calls them to have their sins forgiven. The everlasting blessings we'll receive will be with Him in heaven. Never does Jesus say that being His disciple on this planet will be easy or prosperous.)*

A present-day inheritance. By distorting the Abrahamic Covenant, the Prosperity Gospel proclaims there will be a vast inheritance available in this life. If a person believes in Jesus, he will inherit great possessions and tangible blessings in this life. *(God did promise Abraham that he would inherit the world. This promise was fulfilled with Jesus's advent, ministry, and sacrifice on the cross. The most precious thing Abraham and his descendants could have received was the blessings of salvation, the everlasting inheritance promised by God.)*

Give to get. The way to gain riches in this life is to give more money to the kingdom. The more you give, the more you get. *(Christians do have the duty and privilege of giving generously to the work of God's Kingdom on Earth. This is a response of thanksgiving—for all that He's given us and continues to give us every day. Scripture never teaches us to give in order to gain even more and lay up treasure for ourselves on Earth.)*

Name it and claim it. Faith and prayer allow you to gain control of physical and material blessings in this life. God is standing by to give you money and material blessings if you believe and pray for them. God wants to make you prosperous! *(God is not a cosmic ATM machine. Often, we pray for something not in line with His plans for us and He will, in effect, say "No" or "Later." Paul had an annoying affliction throughout his life and God chose not to heal it, despite earnest prayers. God's plan for you, should you decide to accept His offer of Christ, is to forgive your sin and to lead you on a road of sanctification. Remember that the only perfect person ever was Jesus Christ. When He was crucified, He had no money and He had no possessions—not even a piece of clothing. God wants to save you, not make you wealthy.)*

Why are people drawn to such a message? Maybe they are downtrodden and have no real means or hope of elevating their status in life. Maybe some of the adherents are greedy. Still, others who run these types of churches and ministries are likely to become very wealthy as the donations pour in.

Deism

Deism is a religious philosophy based on the Enlightenment-era thinking, which swept Western civilization during the eighteenth and nineteenth centuries. Enlightenment naïvely assumed that everything could be determined with logic, rational thinking, and the methodologies of scientific inquiry. It basically believes in a Supreme Being, the creator and prime mover of all things. And our interactions with Him, and each other, should use the vehicle of reason. Thus, they systematically oppose anything written in the Bible, which was counter to everyday experiences of human beings. It strongly opposes supernatural occurrences or interactions and treats such narratives as myths or metaphors. The leaders of this movement were European and American who, as a group, were very intelligent, well-educated, and well-spoken. Voltaire, Napoleon Bonaparte, Victor Hugo, Jules Verne, Adam Smith, Thomas Paine, Thomas Jefferson, Benjamin Franklin, and Abraham Lincoln were Deists. In fact, Thomas Jefferson "edited" a Bible to exclude all the miraculous or unexplained events in the Bible. Obviously, the New Testament was a lot smaller and virtually meaningless after his editing.

What are their main beliefs?

A Supreme Being. A supreme being created the universe through force of reason. Deists deny Christ and the Holy Spirit as persons of God, so in a general sense, their faith outwardly resembles Judaism. Their version of God cares for His creation but is not a personal God and primarily intervenes when needed.

Worship. They claim to call for worship of God a.k.a. the Supreme Being. But it's not clear what that worship entails. Many assert that worship is the pursuit of a virtuous life. Some Desists believe in prayer; others do not.

Morality. Virtue is the highest morality. Right living in relationship with fellow human beings is part of that highest ideal.

Repentance. The way to appease God is to grieve over things and thoughts you know are wrong. Desists deny that anything further than repenting for wrongs is required to satisfy God's justice.

Immortality. Desists have differing views about immortality. Some deny the concept. Those who affirm immortality maintain that eternal life is possible if one does right in this life. Heaven is available on a works-of-righteousness basis.

Deism's appeal is twofold: there is no stark choice between accepting God's grace through Christ and rejecting Christ. Jesus, in His own words, does not equivocate on the choices available. And if you try hard and keep your nose clean, the Supreme Being will save you. You see a lot of classical Deism in other traditions including Judaism, Unitarianism, Jehovah's Witnesses, and the Mormons, among others. It's also a popular non-religion among those who profess science or secular humanism as their philosophy of life.

Christianity claims, based on the entirety of the Bible, that God is one but has three persons—the Father, the Son, and the Holy Spirit. Furthermore, God is personally and intimately involved with every aspect of His creation, including us. We worship Him because He is worthy and we are eternally grateful for everything He has blessed us with, including salvation through Jesus Christ. Christianity says that man, by nature, is sinful, not merely prone to making errors of judgment. Good works cannot possibly save us, only the sacrifice of Jesus can.

BRUCE D. WOODS

Legalism and Antinomianism

Legalism and antinomianism can be thought of as two sides of a counterfeit coin.

Legalism basically postulates that keeping the law is the only thing that matters before God. It insists that a person can be accepted by God and His grace, but we remain in His grace on the basis of law-keeping. Legalism often goes hand in hand with works of righteousness. Legalism claims that the good works you do on Earth count against the sin debt you have and are continuing to build. Christ has atoned for your sin, but it's possible to lose your status of being justified by God through His grace *if* you don't do the required good works.

Antinomianism claims that since it is God's grace that saves you, it doesn't really matter how you behave or what, if any, efforts you put forth to obey His commandments. This type of twisted representation of the dynamics of grace and works in one's life led several Christian theologians and entire denominations into "easy-believism," or as Martin Luther called it, "cheap grace." The grace of God which included the sacrifice of His Son on the cross was *not* cheap. The most precious person ever, the perfect Jesus, suffered and died a cruel death to enable that grace. This perversion of Christian doctrine enables people to basically ignore God's laws. It also offers a counterfeit freedom to do whatever you want with unlimited "Get Out of Jail Free" cards.

Yes, it is grace alone that is salvational; our works count for nothing against the unpayable sin debt we owe. But if you are thankful about the enormity of God's gift to you, then you should be impelled to do as He says. We need to reflect God's glory because of what He's done, not because of who we are. Ways to reflect His glory and be thankful include:

- Testify to the wonderful work started within you by the Holy Spirit, Christ's presence and the truth of His written Word.
- Be willing to defend your faith in Him.
- Be a spokesperson for Christ.
- Be a good neighbor and a helpful friend.
- Worship Him in your daily life and as part of the Body of Christ.

Jesus reiterated that He came not to destroy the Law but to fulfill it. Grace is truly important and wonderful, but to live lives reflecting that wonderful gift is pleasing to God.

CHAPTER 6:

Some Western Cults

Jehovah's Witnesses

This cult was started within an isolated Bible study group, which then, over time, developed some very deviant doctrines by Charles Taze Russell. In 1879, this group began publishing the predecessor of what later became *The Watchtower* magazine. Initially, Jehovah's Witnesses were called Zion's Watch Tower Tract Society. Later, as this cult developed through Russell's successor, Joseph Franklin Rutherford, it was renamed Jehovah's Witnesses. The third influential leader of this cult was Nathan Homer Knorr, who added some wrinkles of his own, including a "new translation" of the Bible to be coincident with the major beliefs of the Witnesses. Throughout the history of this cult, it has been forced to deal with many embarrassing, untrue predictions about major events—political and religious—and fulfillments of Bible prophecies. The explanations put forward to explain these failed predictions have certainly been imaginative and sometimes convoluted.

Some of their beliefs include:

- They reject the deity of Jesus. They say He was a god, a mighty god, but He was created by God.
- They reject the Trinity concept as "satanic."
- The Holy Spirit is "God's active force," not a person of God.
- Jesus was raised from the dead as a spiritual creature.
- The atonement of Christ is seen as bringing back perfect human life.
- Jesus returned to Earth in spiritual form in 1914.
- Heaven is Jehovah's reign on Earth with the 144,000 elite and other saved people.

This cult actively recruits and evangelizes. Often, in an initial conversation with a Jehovah's Witness, almost none of their deviant, and obviously non-Christian beliefs, will be mentioned. Their likely recruit—like many cults that actively seek new members—will probably be a person of no faith or a long-forgotten faith associated in their minds with rejection, a family rift, or some other tragedy.

Christian Science

This cult has long been the "queen mother" of the mind-science groups which embrace the gnostic heresy. Others in this group include the Unity School of Christianity and various religious-science/mind-science groups. A central tenet of all these groups is the denial of Jesus's deity.

Christian Science was popularized by Mary Baker Eddy. It offers people a sanctuary from the preaching the Gospel that points out the reality of sin and our corrupted natures.

It's impossible for an honest Christian to be self-righteous. This cult denies the existence of evil. And if there is no evil then repentance and salvation are irrelevant. These new "truths" are not found in the Bible; they are found through writings such as Eddy's book, *Science and Health with Key to the Scriptures*.

Mary Ann Morse Baker was born in 1821. She was sickly as a child and didn't enjoy a happy childhood. She married her first husband, George Glover, at twenty-one. Glover soon caught yellow fever and died, leaving Baker a pregnant widow. Ten years later, she married Daniel Patterson, a dentist, whom she later divorced. Her third marriage was to Asa G. Eddy, a student and self-pronounced practitioner of Christian Science. Mary Baker Eddy became a widow again when Eddy died of a chronic heart condition. Mary caused quite a stir when she claimed her husband was killed by arsenic poisoning. Her "witness" for this diagnosis was later imprisoned for illegal medical practices.

Already familiar with Christian Science, Mary Baker Eddy mixed these teachings with some from Phineas Parkhurst Quimby to form her "new revelation." This mix was the basis for her book. Quimby sued Eddy, claiming that she had pirated his ideas and teachings. But Eddy's version of events was backed by the growing movement and the well-received book, and Quimby's claims were dismissed.

Mary Baker Eddy made bold claims about her healing abilities and accomplishments. When challenges were issued by doctors or clergy, she ignored them and never discussed them publicly. Later in life when seriously ill, she secretly utilized medical doctors instead of relying on Christian Science practitioners.

Christian Science has several tenets in their belief system, which include:

- Ideals are realities and internal forces are primary causes.
- Mind is primary and causative while matter is secondary.
- People are spiritual citizens of a divine universe.
- The remedy for all defect and disorder is metaphysical (focusing on "first principles" such as existence, causality, truth).
- God is imminent (inherent) — a divine principle.
- Humanity is divine.
- Truth is revealed progressively to every new generation.
- Mankind can be free from the necessity of belief in disease.
- Our real search is the discovery of our soul.
- Evil has no place in the plan of God and there is no future punishment (hell).

This cult used to be far more influential than it is now. The *Christian Science Monitor* used to be a world-class newspaper. Christian Science Reading Rooms still exist all over the USA. But, it has been rocked by scandals and infighting and people are more cognizant that the utilization of modern medicine is not anti-Christian or anti-religious any more than utilizing modern farming or manufacturing technologies. As in the breakfast cereal "Grape-Nuts," which, though delicious, is neither grape nor nuts, Christian Science has long since been proven to be neither Christian nor science.

Mormons/Church of Jesus Christ LDS

The main body of the Mormons is called the Church of Jesus Christ of Latter-day Saints—this is the Utah-based branch. The largest smaller group is called the Community of Christ (formerly the Reorganized Church of Latter-day Saints)—this branch is Missouri-based. This group was the brainchild of Joseph Smith Jr.

A bit of background is required to understand Smith. He was born in Vermont and his father was a shiftless grifter who sold maps to Captain Kidd's buried treasure, used "peep stones" to tell fortunes, along with other con games and scams. The family moved around and was, by reputation, irreligious and whiskey-drinking. Smith's autobiography includes his family being members of the Presbyterian Church, but no such record or independent verification was ever found. Per the testimony of other community members, Smith and his family were considered liars and without moral character.

At the age of fourteen, Smith claimed he had a vision while walking in the woods near Palmyra, New York, in 1820. Two personages appeared before him, and one said the other was their "beloved son"—presumably one was God, and one was Jesus. Smith asked God what sect or branch of the church to join, and God said, "None of them, because they are all corrupt and hypocritical."

Later, in 1823, he had another vision, of a messenger of God, Moroni, who gave Smith a job to do. He was to "translate" the gospel, as it had been delivered by Jesus, to the inhabitants of the Western Hemisphere. To aid Smith in his translation of "the golden plates," the Urim and Purim stones were to be used—they would be found with the plates. He was told where the plates were but also told not to take them for four years. Smith apparently took possession of the plates and stones in 1827 and translated the plates, publishing the translation in 1830.

The five golden plates were never seen by any others — except for Smith and the eight witnesses vouching for the Book of Mormon. Five of those witnesses were in one family (Whitmer) and three were in Smith's family. Three of these witnesses later left the Mormon church.

Smith, now married, moved to Pennsylvania and wrote another book, *Doctrine and Covenants*. Smith also began work on a revision of the King James Version Bible, which included a new section in Genesis chapter 50 to predict his own appearance. It was in Pennsylvania that Smith and close associate Oliver Cowdery became priests in their new religion. John the Baptist supposedly descended and conferred on them the "Priesthood of Aaron," and later Peter, James, and John conferred on them the "Priesthood of Melchizedek."

Smith and his followers were increasingly running afoul of the law, preaching polygamy along with expounding his new religion that was becoming increasingly anti-Christian. Forced out of Pennsylvania, they moved to Ohio, then Missouri, then Illinois. Smith also penned a third volume of Mormonism, *The Pearl of Great Price*.

Now espousing religious views far outside the mainstream, they again ran afoul of the law as they tried to destroy the presses of a local newspaper that was critical of the new religion. Joseph and brother Hyrum were jailed in Nauvoo, Illinois. Using guns smuggled into the jail, the Smiths and the mob that attacked the jail were involved in a shootout. The Smith brothers were killed but not before several attackers were shot by them. The actual account doesn't match the Mormon historical account whereby the Smiths were "martyred for their faith."

Most of the Mormons then migrated to Utah, led by Brigham Young. A smaller group led by Smith's widow and his son moved to Missouri. The main group in Utah practiced polygamy and brutally enforced their will on non-Mormons, and, for many years, held an iron-fisted grip on the local and territorial governments. It required the US Army's intervention to break the tyranny of the Mormon rule in Utah, which had legalized polygamy—often little better than the slavery of women starting as early as age fourteen. There are still some rogue Mormon sects in the western US that practice polygamy and ignore secular civil government authority.

This cult has many deviant beliefs, and even its own doctrinal books aren't consistent with each other. A snapshot of their sacred books and belief system is noted:

- The Bible—King James Version for Utah Mormons, Revised/Smith version for Missouri Mormons—and the Book of Mormon, *Doctrine and Covenants*, and *The Pearl of Great Price* are all considered sacred books.
  - The Book of Mormon (supposedly translated from "Reformed Egyptian"—no such language ever existed) is fiction. Its two primary sources are plagiarized and/or edited passages from the King James Version Bible and Solomon Spaulding's unpublished novel, *Manuscript Found*. It includes many errors, impossibilities, and anachronisms.
  - *Doctrine and Covenants* is a complete Smith invention. It includes theological blessings for concepts such as baptism of the dead, celestial marriage, and

polygamy. Several items in this book contradict Smith's other works and, of course, the Bible.
  - *The Pearl of Great Price* is Smith's third work supposedly translated from Egyptian papyri. Smith revealed he'd been divinely given the ability to translate from Egyptian. Later, the papyri used were translated by experts and found to be primarily burial instructions; *not one word* from these papyri was translated accurately by Smith.
- Mormons deny the Trinity and the deity of Jesus Christ. God is not a spiritual being. He impregnated Eve (one of His celestial wives) to start the human race. Jesus became a God and an example for all mankind. Jesus was conceived by a union between Adam/God and Mary. We, as humans, can also become gods just like Jesus did. Jesus was a polygamist having been married to Mary, Martha, and Mary Magdalene. The Holy Spirit was also begotten of God through a goddess wife.
- Salvation is based on good works not just faith in Jesus.
- Atonement is the resurrection of the human body for a continuing life of connubial bliss.
- Jesus and Lucifer were pre-existent brothers.
- All souls pre-existed in heaven and it is the duty of humans to have as many children as possible to speed up the cycling of souls through humanity by which they can become gods and go to the highest level of heaven.
- There are three levels of heaven: telestial, terrestrial, and celestial.

What is truly bizarre about this belief system is that, despite multiple, significant inconsistencies within the framework of Mormonism, with the tenets as stated in the three Smith books and the Bible, it has become a popular, powerful, and growing faith. It is both wealthy and influential. The primary emphasis among Mormons is behavior. Mormons are not to drink alcoholic or caffeinated beverages. The family is strongly emphasized as is moral and ethical behavior. Mormons strongly support their church with tithes and personal service—two-year sabbaticals for missionary work are common for high school graduates. But as Christians know, through biblical teaching, good works are *not* salvational—only the grace of God through Jesus Christ can save us from the consequences of our sins.

Unitarian/Universalist

This set of beliefs—or non-beliefs—can be traced as far back as the first century AD, ever since the leaders of the Jewish hierarchy denied the evidence and eye-witness testimony about Jesus Christ. This cult denies the nature of Jesus and closely resembles the Deist view of the universe. In the USA, Unitarianism was founded by Jonathan Mayhew and Charles Chauncey. They were associated with Harvard and helped change Harvard from a Christian (Congregational) school to a secular institution. Later, William Channing helped form the American Unitarian Association. The group then merged with the Universalist movement and is now the Unitarian Universalist Association. It's easy to become a Unitarian—they have no central doctrines and there is very little to believe in. At a church service, the themes are often truth, nature, beauty, and service to each other. Familiar Christian hymns frequently have new lyrics that don't mention God, Christ, the Holy Spirit, etc. The guiding principles seem to be "get along with your neighbor" and "try to live a moral and good life." Per their "live and let live" philosophy, they tolerate casual drug use, homosexual relationships and marriage, and other behaviors that Christians might find offensive or deem sinful. What they do believe includes:

- They reject the Bible as a sacred text.
- Belief in God may be, for them, a personal God, a God concept, or no God at all.
- They do not believe in any aspect of Jesus beyond His being a wise teacher.
- They believe in the perfectibility of humanity through their own efforts.
- They deny there are absolute rights and wrongs; situations dictate acceptable behavior.
- There is no heaven or hell.

The Unitarians seem to be well-intentioned people but their church offers no more than a focus for social gatherings and, perhaps, a support group for those in need.

Scientology

This group was founded in the 1950s by L. Ron Hubbard. As the son of a navy officer, he spent a good bit of his youth in the Far East. He returned to the US in 1930 to attend college and flunked out; he later bought a phony PhD degree from "Sequoia University" which operated out of an LA post office box. Hubbard moved from job to job until WWII. While in the navy, he was shipwrecked and severely injured. He supposedly regained perfect health by applying his self-discovered principles of Scientology.

After the war, Hubbard started writing fiction, primarily science-fiction stories. He was good at this genre and continued to write until 1986. He also started developing his "principles of dianetics" and published a book about them in 1950. It was immediately popular. *Dianetics: The Modern Science of Mental Health* is a do-it-yourself psychoanalysis manual. Hubbard claimed that most major problems are caused by prenatal experiences. Not long after his book came out, it was attacked by medical, psychiatric, and legal experts as being complete nonsense and an intent to defraud the public. Of course, it was and is nonsense. Hubbard then turned this lucrative enterprise from "self-help psychoanalysis" to a "religion," thus gaining protection from the law to keep on selling his dianetics hokum. Scientology became a new religion.

As a religion, Hubbard emulated Far East religions with "levels of attainment." Per expensive dianetics "studies" and "experiences," one can progress through the many ranks of Scientology toward ultimate enlightenment. Some points about Scientology include:

- Jesus was just another great teacher, like Buddha, etc.
- There is no sin.
- God may or may not exist.
- Reincarnation sufficiently explains man's existence but Scientology is the freedom from reincarnation.
- Man is basically good and will evolve to become a godlike "Homo novus."

Scientology is not good medicine, good ethics, good philosophy, nor even good religion. But Scientology, for the late L. Ron Hubbard and his followers was good for business. It is still a profitable scam today.

BRUCE D. WOODS

Unification Church

The Korean-born Sun Myung Moon founded this church and his followers were known for decades as "moonies." Born in 1920, he was raised as a Presbyterian, though he was influenced early in life by mysticism. At sixteen, Moon supposedly had a vision in which Jesus appeared and told Moon he had an important mission to accomplish. What this mission supposedly was is unclear. Some accounts say Moon was to be the Second Coming of Christ. Other accounts say that Moon was to prepare for Christ's Second Coming.

Moon went to college in Japan and, while there, developed "The Divine Principle." In 1945, Moon began to preach—his teachings were primarily a mixture of deviant fundamental Christianity and anti-communism.

During this time, he ran afoul of the law, accumulating bigamy and adultery charges. He was sentenced to three years in a labor camp. Afterward, Moon moved back to Korea and founded his church in 1954. Though preaching chastity and the sanctity of marriage, Moon often faced charges of sexual misconduct and ritual sex practices. In 1955, the Presbyterian Church of Korea branded Moon a heretic for three reasons: (1) Moon placed himself above Jesus as the object of faith, (2) Moon's doctrines violated the morals of modern society, and (3) his church was engaged in deceptive recruiting and evangelistic practices. In 1972, Moon moved to the USA and founded the American branch of his Unification Church. Moon's messages and doctrines included these variant beliefs:

- There have been three Adams. The first was supposed to have married Eve and have perfect children,

but Eve was sexually seduced by Lucifer. The second was Jesus who was to marry and have children but, somehow, John the Baptist failed Jesus and Jesus's mission went unfulfilled. Then God allowed Jesus to die to attain "spiritual salvation" for man. Not having a wife, Jesus was given the (female) Holy Spirit. Moon claimed that a third Adam was now required to perfectly complete God's plan of redemption. (Any ideas that Moon was the third Adam disappeared with Moon's death in 2012.)
- Jesus was not divine, just a perfect man.
- The Bible is insufficient for salvation without The Divine Principle as applied in the Unification church.

The Unification church owns several businesses and large tracts of real estate but does little in terms of charitable work and outreach to the poor. The grossly distorted doctrines offered by this cult shouldn't fool many Christians—unless they are both ignorant and foolish.

New Age

It's a toss-up whether New Ageism should be considered a cult or occult group. However, since much of the several variants within this overall heading don't act primarily in secret or imply that they have hidden truths that can be only discovered within the group, I chose to label it a cult. The New Age movement is an amalgam of several inputs, including many ancient occult groups, eastern religions, theosophy, Native American beliefs, etc. Many New Age adherents do follow one or more occultic beliefs—occultic practices are also common for the more dedicated followers. New Age is more of a repackaging effort of old religions, pagan practices, and beliefs deemed heretical by the early Christian church. It's more of a movement and lifestyle guide than it is a standard laundry list of beliefs and practices. Very few non-Christian or anti-Christian beliefs are excluded from being a part of this toxic recipe. Some of what they believe is:

- God is not a personal being, it is a creative force. God may be thought of as a father-mother-child.
- The Trinity is substituted by "Eternal Thought," which consists of intelligence and force.
- Jesus was only an enlightened teacher.
- Atonement is not required. Salvation is accomplished by good works and reincarnation.
- There is no absolute truth.

The New Age movement is yet another movement started and supported by Satan—the usual threefold tenets of a cult being the denial of the Bible as the Word of God, denial of Jesus as fully divine, and belief that good works and self-improvement are salvational. New Age often seems to be joyous, fun, campy, and the odd clothing and Eastern-based music often seem exotic or even attractive, but it promotes the same old lies through the same old adversary.

CHAPTER 7

Two Groups in Transition

Grace Communion International
(formerly Worldwide Church of God)

This church was founded by the late Herbert W. Armstrong. For most of its history, this church was definitely a cult—and an influential one at that. This cult, during Armstrong's leadership (before the church later rejected the cultic tenets of Armstrongism), once held several errant beliefs, including:

- The Bible is God's Word but was best interpreted by Armstrong, who anointed himself as God's apostle.
- Jesus and the Father are two gods of the "God Family."
- The Trinity was rejected. Jesus became a god and the Holy Spirit is not a person of God.
- The resurrection of Jesus was spiritual, not physical.
- Salvation is the result of good works and Christ's sacrifice.

- Mankind becomes a God Being and part of the God Family after salvation.

Armstrong's theology borrowed from the Mormons, Jehovah's Witnesses, Seventh-Day Adventists, and two books which Armstrong was heavily influenced by—John Wilson's *Our Israelitish Heritage* and Edward Hines's *The Identification of the British Nation with the Lost Tribes of Israel*. These books convinced Armstrong that Britain and the US were the lost tribes of Ephraim and Manasseh. This postulate has never been taken seriously by biblical scholars or reputable historians but they greatly influenced Armstrong and how he interpreted the prophecies of the Bible. The church grew and prospered under Armstrong despite a falling out between himself and his son, Garner Ted Armstrong, who split with his father to form his own version of the church.

However, after Armstrong died in 1986, the leaders of the church accomplished a remarkable thing: they repudiated Armstrong, non-Christian beliefs, and the church is now a member of the National Association of Evangelicals. The cult Armstrong fabricated from Christianity and other sources was remade into a Christian denomination! It formally renamed itself in 2009 to become Grace Communion International. It will be interesting to follow this re-tooled, newly Christian denomination and see what happens.

Seventh-Day Adventists

This group has an interesting past and is engaged in a struggle to either strengthen its Christian footings or spiral down into cultism through its doctrines and bases for beliefs that are at odds with orthodox Christianity.

Currently, the consensus is that they are a branch of the Christian church but the struggles continue among the Adventists for its soul. Certainly, many Adventists are truly Christian despite some heterodox concepts that the Adventists still hold.

This movement started in 1844, and as the nineteenth century progressed, Adventism captured the imagination of many churchgoers. A Baptist pastor, William Miller assumed a leading role in the Adventist movement. There were high and growing expectations of Jesus's Second Coming. However, despite biblical admonitions—that we are not to know when—predictions were made, and then the predictors had to explain away why they didn't come true. (Predicting the Second Coming was also a major activity of the Jehovah's Witnesses born in the same era.) This emphasis on predicting the Second Coming became known as "Millerism."

Miller and his followers disbanded but Adventism continued. Three separate groups fused to become the Seventh-Day Adventists. Prophecy and teachings focused on the Second Coming dominated this new church.

Early in the theological development of this new group, an Adventist adherent joined—Ellen Harmon (later White). She profoundly affected the church's development. She experienced her first vision in 1844, subsequently had more visions, and wrote several influential books concerning the faith, Jesus, her visions, etc. She was a prolific author; perhaps her most influential book is *The Desire of Ages*, depicting the life and ministry of Christ.

The problem with Ellen White in this church is the reverence and status attached to her writings by the church. She has been deemed by the Adventists to have received the "Spirit of Prophesy." And therefore, some

Adventists view her writings as sacred and supplementary material for the Bible. This is obviously contentious in orthodox Christianity. Additionally, the Adventists hold some unorthodox views on some other aspects of the Christian faith. Some of their beliefs are:

- Seventh-day—Saturday—worship services.
- Strict observance of kosher food laws—they recommend vegetarianism.
- Belief in the primacy of the Bible, though Mrs. White's writings are held in high regard.
- They believe that hell is "soul-sleep." The non-conscious state of death is "separation from God" until the saved are raised from the dead.
- Their Holy Communion rite adds foot-washing to the eating of bread and drinking of wine.
- Their version of atonement is a variant of "the sin-bearer" and Christ's present work in Heaven.
- Salvation is given through God's grace but requires good works as well—similar to the Roman Catholic viewpoint. (By the way, James's epistle is often misunderstood about the grace and works discussions.)

Adventists seem willing to reinforce that the Bible is their one authoritative source of faith and doctrine, and they continue to wrestle with positions that could be modified to match generally accepted orthodoxy. I would call this church group a "sect"—per my earlier definitions—within the Christian church but it is not a cult.

CHAPTER 8

Some Eastern Cults

Zen Buddhism

This is the most popular form of the three main branches of Buddhism in the West but classical Buddhism has won over some celebrity adherents and is in the news frequently with the extremely overhyped Dalai Lama. (The leader of the Tibetan Buddhists seems to be little more than an "advocate" of Tibetan independence and a figurehead for Buddhism.)

Buddhism started as a reaction to the oppression of Hinduism in India. With Hinduism, the vast majority of the poverty-stricken masses were doomed thanks to the caste system—an endless and hopeless cycle of incarnations with no hope for the future. Buddhism offered hope with a new system of thoughts and new "understandings."

Gautama Buddha offered the masses the hope for Nirvana, an undefined state of being. He presented the four noble truths: existence is pain; the cause of suffering is desire; when suffering is destroyed, passions must also be destroyed to gain a state of bliss; and removing suffering is a process of moral cultivation, included in the eightfold path—right views of the four noble truths, right intention, right speech, right action, right livelihood, right effort, right usefulness, and right concentration.

Zen Buddhism, popularized in the West with the hippies and, subsequently, is a variant of Buddhism with these beliefs, many of which are shared across Buddhist groups:

- Zen is at once the knower and the known. It's supposedly a way to the truth.
- Zen has nothing to offer (re: intellectual analysis). Followers may have a set of doctrines but they are not from Zen. Zen, per se, has no cardinal doctrines.
- Communication with God is through one's eye and God's eye—they become one and the same.
- Zen consciousness is a mind-made oneness with life.
- Good and evil are opposites just as light and dark, etc.
- Zen is about freeing one's consciousness and loving oneself—first, last, and always.
- The reason people suffer is because their desires are fixated on the illusion of self.

Clearly, Buddhism in any form, including the Zen variant, cannot be mistaken as a road to God or a way to be saved from the consequences of sin and evil.

Bahá'í

This faith dates back to 1844, when a Persian named Mullá Husayn started searching for a messiah. He met a young man—Siyyid 'Alí-Muhammad of Shiraz—who convinced Mullá that he (Siyyid) was the "Báb," the "Gate of

God." This Báb was to be the manifestation of God and a herald of a greater messenger to come. Alas, the Báb was arrested in 1850, charged with sedition and "anti-Islamic activity" and was shot to death. One of his followers, Mízrá Husayn 'Ali Núrí, was supposedly informed by an angel that he was to assume the name "Bahá'u'lláh"—the glory and splendor of God. (Modest, wasn't he?)

He became the hero to the Bábi's and wrote the Bahá'í scriptures. He announced that he was the "promised one." He took control of the movement amid family infighting and, despite his claim of immortality, died in 1892. Many of the faithful moved to the US in the early twentieth century—partly to escape persecution by Islam forces in Persia and elsewhere.

This cult, invented from whole cloth, has a hodge-podge of beliefs, including:

- The Bible is a sacred book but the final authority is the writings of Bahá'u'lláh.
- Bahá'u'lláh is one of the nine great messiahs of the world, which include Jesus, Buddha, Muhammad, etc.
- God is one person only.
- Salvation is based upon good works coupled with God's mercy.

The Bahá'í offer a mushy blend of peace, love, justice, and obedience without the need to engage any critical thinking skills or doing any research about the basis for one's beliefs. They purport to be a nonjudgmental blend of the best of the major faiths. For the lonely, lost, or disenfranchised being a part of this affirming group might offer a temporary balm.

BRUCE D. WOODS

Hare Krishna (ISKCON/TM)

Gone are the days when virtually every major airport was a focus of this offshoot of Hinduism with their literature giveaways—donations accepted, of course—and their blatant recruitment appeals. Hooray for that!

This was the brainchild of A. C. Bhaktivedanta Swami in the early 1960s. This "guru" actively recruited young people, primarily from the hippies, commune members, pot smokers, and dropouts. He gave them a role, a purpose, a sense of belonging and success.

This cult emphasizes love and brotherhood. The Beatles' George Harrison wrote a pop song about them, "My Sweet Lord" (listen for the background response "Hare Krishna" during the song).

Hinduism has its own "trinity"—Brahma (creator), Vishnu (preserver), and Shiva (destroyer). The story of Krishna is the "Bhagavad Gita," an eighteen-chapter poem. The Gita itself is part of ninety thousand double verses. In this fable, Krishna is said to have had sixteen thousand wives, etc. Some key tenets of ISKCON are:

- God is an incarnation of Krishna.
- Jesus is but one son of Krishna—not divine.
- Salvation is granted only with perfection through improvement and multiple reincarnations toward Nirvana.
- Transcendental meditation, through Hindu and ISKCON, is a means of losing one's personality in God's. (This is quite different from the concept of Christian meditation and its objectives.)

After some of the leaders of this movement were expelled from the US, the movement has lost momentum and their funding sources have dried up. But there is still a lot of curiosity about Eastern religions and some of those will literally risk their lives for "new experiences."

CHAPTER 9

Some Occult Groups

Kabbalah

This occult set of beliefs is not easily defined. It ostensibly uses the Hebrew Bible—primarily the Torah—as its basis but its real objective is to somehow glean the hidden knowledge of the Torah, access the supernatural powers of God, and use those powers to transform themselves and the world around them. It's a grouping of sects that dabble in Jewish mysticism. Often this dabbling is devoid of religious overtones and focuses on infusing power within themselves.

The three primary groups are the Judaic, Hermetic, and Hollywood sects. All claim to be authentic adherents with legitimate teachers. Of course, one can only learn Kabbalah through officially sanctioned teachers. All groups agree that the Torah is metaphorical. It is not to be taken literally. This approach is constant throughout their studies of the Hebrew Bible/Old Testament.

The myriad complexities of this bizarre occult group are beyond casual discussions. To even be able to discuss parts of their beliefs requires learning a new vocabulary and new meanings to words you think you already know. Some of what they believe is:

- Kabbalah denies the deity of Jesus Christ and most aspects of His being the Messiah.
- Salvation is not necessary—all mistakes are atoned for through Kabbalah study or reincarnation.
- The Hermetic sect is based on a different interpretation of the Hebrew Bible.
- The Hollywood sect combines Judaic with some Hermetic and some New Age ideas.

The Kabbalah occult sects are completely non-Christian even as they make a mockery of the Hebrew Bible. Only minds stuck in neutral could be possible converts to this mush.

Astrology

Many newspapers carry an astrology column. You can buy books about it and get "readings" by phone, by mail, in person, or on the internet. The supposition of this occult tool of Satan is that the time of year—which correlates to the positions of the stars and planets in the night sky—and your birthday somehow influences who you are and your future. Obviously, there has never been a scintilla of evidence to support such a nonsensical claim. Yet millions read the columns and countless thousands let astrology guide and interfere with their lives.

It is often viewed as a "harmless pastime" but it is a serious and dangerous occult-belief system. It usurps God's authority over your life—if you allow it. It was rightly called an abomination in the Old Testament, and Paul warns both the Galatians and the Colossians to stay away from it. Paul called it bondage.

Satanism

Satanism was once rarely brought up in polite company and the very thought of it made people shudder. But since the 1960s, Satanism has made a comeback. In the movie, *Rosemary's Baby*, the self-styled high priest of San Francisco's First Church of Satan, Anton Szandor LaVey, played the role of the devil. The movie was a publicity bonanza for Satanism. There isn't anything subtle about the message of this group—it's 100 percent anti-Christ. Some of what they believe includes:

- Indulgence/satisfaction of one's desires.
- Living for the moment.
- Refusing to be bound by antiquated laws or old-fashioned morals.
- Vengeance, casting aside inhibitions for pleasure or fun, etc.
- Sexual rites, nudity, and drug usage are often part of Satanic rituals.
- Satan wants people to act like unenlightened animals. Satan wants people to ignore God's Commandments.
- Satan wants us to think of ourselves first and others later.

In short, Satan wants us to behave the opposite of what Christ would do. Satanic worship services—the Black Mass—attempt to denigrate and defile every aspect of Christian worship—often by doing the opposite or reading something backward. Blessings are replaced by curses; prayers are replaced by blasphemies. Satanism offers freedom from guilt or responsibility for your actions. A Christian must be grateful that, despite worldly temptations, we have not lost our faith in Jesus Christ and our sure hope for eternal life with Him.

Witchcraft/Wicca

This is not a suitable subject for comic books, cartoons, TV sitcoms, or even something often joked about—especially in late October. This is a very old and still dangerous occult group. It is the use of magical or supernatural powers for anti-social ends—a.k.a. evil purposes.

Where do witches get that power? It's not from God so it must be from another source—Satan. This Old Religion, as it's sometimes called, predates Christianity and is based partly on Greek and Roman mythology. It's a "nature religion" and thus often includes sexual rituals and drug use during some of its ceremonies. Sometimes you hear of "black magic" and "white magic" with witchcraft practices that are evil or good. But when you allow Satan to take control of you and give you supernatural power, the expectation is that you're receiving it to do his bidding.

The Bible condemns witchcraft as an abomination to the Lord. The only supernatural power you want in your life is the power from the Holy Spirit—not the power from the evil one.

Rosicrucianism

This group qualifies as being both an occult group and a secret society. Its supposed basis was a book, about a symbolic character named Christian Rosenkreuz, entitled *Farna*

Fraternitatis. Rosenkreuz was supposedly born in 1378 and died in 1484. He was educated in a monastery and traveled throughout the Holy Land, Egypt, Spain, and finally Austria. He founded the Order of the Rosicrucians. The plot of the book is Rosenkreuz trying to shed light on the "misunderstood" Christian religion and explain the mystery of life. He also tried to use occult practices to explain how religion and science would be harmonized. (Both Rosenkreuz and Rosicrucian translate as Rose Cross.)

The author of the book, Johann Valentin Andrea, intended the book as satire. However, it was used as a basis for a secret society founded hundreds of years later. It was introduced into the US in the 1800s and subsequently split into two groups—Rosicrucians and Ancient Mystical Order Rosae Crucis (AMORC).

They both believe a hodge-podge of peculiar things including:

- Use of other books (e.g., "The Secret Schools") to interpret the scriptures.
- Denial of the deity of Christ or His atonement.
- Denial of sin.
- Salvation by good works.
- Belief in reincarnation (man is evolving into a divine being).

This secret society/occult group offers a Christian nothing—except a life without Christ.

Spiritism

This occult group also is often labeled as Spiritualism. It is well known based on its depictions of séances and rites whereby people supposedly communicate with the dead, but that's just part of this occult group's beliefs. In recent times, spiritism has gotten a boost from quasi-scientific articles and inquiries into such things as ESP, telekinesis, telepathy, and other phenomena associated with the quasi-science called parapsychology.

There are some legitimate universities with parapsychology departments—some are tax-payer supported through taxes and grant monies. However, it is, of course, true that some people have exhibited supernatural powers and abilities that cannot be readily explained. In biblical history, God gave otherwise unremarkable people extraordinary and unexplainable powers for His purposes. So the seduction of being able to find, develop, and use supernatural powers remains. It is tempting to seek those powers and abilities regardless of who is giving them to you or for what purpose. And when it suits Satan's purposes, he will give a person supernatural powers far beyond human explanation.

Beyond pure scientific inquiry, the spiritism movement is based on these seven principles:

1. Fatherhood of God.
2. Brotherhood of man.
3. Continuous existence.
4. Communion of spirits and ministry of angels.
5. Personal responsibility.
6. Compensation and retribution hereafter for good or evil done on Earth.
7. A path of endless progression.

Theosophy

This occult group has its basis in the old gnostic heresy. Once known as Divine Wisdom, it is a mix of spiritism,

Hinduism, Buddhism, and Gnosticism. It was founded by Helena Petrova Blavatsky in 1875. Her successor in 1891 was Annie Besant, a woman involved with radical political movements. She claimed that her adopted son, Krishnamurti, was the "new messiah" or the reincarnation of the "world teacher." This pronouncement happened in 1928. In 1931, Krishnamurti became convinced he was not the messiah and refused further adoration. Despite this apparent setback, Theosophy survived and still exists. Some of what they believe is:

- God is all, all is God.
- Continuous evolutionary cycles of the universe.
- Reincarnation.
- Fourfold nature of a person—mental body, physical body with its etheric double, and an astral body.
- The Law of Causation (Karma).
- The preexistence of souls.
- Self-salvation.

Theosophy is a combination of invalid beliefs wrapped inside a secret society. A mixture of poisons like these couldn't be beneficial for anyone!

CHAPTER 10

Some Facts about Islam

Islam (translates to mean "submission") is the second-largest religion in the world and, of the major religions, by far the fastest-growing. It encompasses not only its own fundamental scripture basis—The Qur'an—but it also paints a portrait of a supreme being who is fundamentally different (in several ways) than the God of the Hebrews and Christians.

Their description and beliefs about the chief prophet of Islam, Muhammad, are also significantly at odds with the person and attributes of Jesus Christ. Additionally, Islam sets forth a peculiar legal system that is supposedly in accordance with the prophecies of Muhammad, which they put forth as a substitute for the legal basis of Western civilization and the concept of not comingling the church and state due to the probable corruption of both the religion and the government. The enlightened view that society must protect both religions from the state and the state from a dominant religion is not shared by Islam.

One of the current dialogues among Christians, Jews, and Muslims—presumably operating with goodwill and friendly intentions—includes discussions that might lead to characterize the Hebrew-Christian God as being the same supreme being (separated by idioms, translations, misunderstandings, etc.) as Islam's Allah (from the word *el-ah*, meaning "a god"). However, attempts to accommodate or harmonize two far different concepts of a supreme being cannot succeed unless one or both viewpoints of God are blurred or compromised for the sake of peace, goodwill, or harmony.

Some think that glossing over the differences between God and Allah would be useful for "further dialogue" or "the sake of peace." I do not share that viewpoint. I think that true peace and harmony come by recognizing there are actual differences in our faiths and not letting those differences lead to conflict. Further understanding, education, and exploring new ways to work together for the common good should be among the primary objectives in interfaith dialogues. Our foundational beliefs should not be subjects for negotiation or accommodation by secularism or "popular" opinion.

(See the attachments for more about Islam. There are many websites with objective, fact-based comparisons of Islam versus Christianity, etc. Feel free to consult them; I've listed a couple in the bibliography.)

CHAPTER 11

Christianity and Secret Societies

There are many secret societies: certain college fraternities and sororities, lodges, societies with certain membership criteria, etc. They number into the hundreds in the US alone. The issue for Christians becomes when a secret society's beliefs are in conflict with basic Christian beliefs.

The Bible is clear that we cannot serve two masters. Therefore, it is impossible to swear an oath to believe in and act in accordance with a set of society's beliefs if they are at odds with your Christian faith. It's *not* okay to be a "good Christian" on Sunday morning and a "good ___ society/lodge member" on Tuesday night *if* the society's beliefs are anti-Christian. Many secret societies are syncretic—offering an amalgam of Christian or Judeo-Christian beliefs welded to a special, secret set of beliefs, which are often based on myth, legends, etc., and are not biblical. Many societies also denigrate or ignore Jesus, casting Him as a wise man or prophet but denying that He was the Son of God. One famous (and popular for their good works) adjunct of a secret society openly uses Eastern religious garb and terminology inconsistent with Christian beliefs.

Many secret societies are not anti-Christian and their oaths, pledges, and expected behavior won't put a Christian in a compromising position. But there are also many societies that do have beliefs that someone joining them must take an oath to uphold *and* keep secret. Their non-Christian beliefs are often not apparent until one is already a member.

The main attraction of becoming a member often has to do with social status and the benefits of being part of a strong and influential support group, regardless of what they might believe. And despite the fact many secret society pledges, oaths, and the details of their beliefs have long since been revealed and published, many people are ignorant of societal beliefs that are not Christian.

If you are a Christian, it's a wise practice to not belong to groups with viewpoints that are opposed to or inconsistent with the basic tenets of the Christian faith. Good works—regardless of the organization sponsoring them—are not sufficient nor are they salvational!

CONCLUSION

Dos and Don'ts

Do not "debate" with a cult member—continue to firmly but calmly express your beliefs and the biblical basis for them. *They* are well-rehearsed and often utilize out-of-context, deviant Scripture translations or misinterpretations of Bible passages. They often utilize distorted terminology for their beliefs as well as non-biblical sources.

Do not pay for any "literature" they give you or contribute to any cause they might be representing. If they leave you with any material, please be careful with it—you wouldn't want to give an erroneous impression to a household member or a guest that you support or are sympathetic to their belief system.

When interacting with a cult member, do let the love of Jesus Christ shine through you. Let the glory of God be reflected by you. Your behavior can be a powerful witness for Jesus and your faith. Remember that it is the Holy Spirit's job to bring people to Christ—our job is to be His witness and share the Good News.

What We Can Learn From Cults

- It is important to have definite convictions about matters of faith.

- It is important to share your faith.
- It is important to use the media to get your message across.
- It is important to impart a sense of urgency.
- It is important for laypeople to be involved in church work.
- It is important to know the Bible and the biblical basis for your belief.
- It is important to be dedicated.
- It is important to learn to witness and testify about your faith.
- It is important to be able to endure ridicule.
- It is important to our well-being to practice our faith.

Snapshot Evaluation of Some Cult Beliefs

Through the fifteen (as I have parsed it in the introduction) basic beliefs that most Christians share, the seven Western cult systems, seen in chapter six, are evaluated against those fifteen beliefs. The summary is noted on the attached spreadsheet. Eastern cults, apostate religions, and occult groups rarely believe even one of the basic Christian beliefs. These groups are readily distinguished as non-Christian. For Christians, the primary challenge remains that these groups either represent themselves as Christian or may be viewed as Christian by the media and the uninformed.

APPENDIX A

Important Christian Councils

Council	Date	Convoked by	Led by	Attendance (approx.)	Topics
First Council of Nicaea	May 20–June 19, AD 325	Emperor Constantine I	Hosius of Corduba (and Emperor Constantine)	318	Arianism, the nature of Christ; celebration of Passover (Easter); ordination of eunuchs; prohibition of kneeling on Sundays and from Easter to Pentecost; validity of baptism by heretics, lapsed Christians; sundry other matters
First Council of Constantinople	May–July, AD 381	Emperor Theodosius I	Timothy of Alexandria, Meletius of Antioch, Gregory Nazianzus, and Nectarius of Constantinople	150	Arianism; Apollinarism; Sabellianism; Holy Spirit; successor to Meletius
Council of Ephesus	June 22–July 31, AD 431	Emperor Theodosius II	Cyril of Alexandria	200–250	Nestorianism; Theotokos; Pelagianism
Council of Chalcedon	Oct. 8–Nov. 1, AD 451	Emperor Marcian	A board of government officials and senators led by the patrician Anatolius	520	The judgments issued at the Second Council of Ephesus in 449; the alleged offenses of Bishop Dioscorus of Alexandria;

					the relationship between the divinity and humanity of Christ; many disputes involving particular bishops and sees
Second Council of Constantinople	May 5–June 2, AD 553	Emperor Justinian I	Eutychius of Constantinople	152	Nestorianism; Origenism
Third Council of Constantinople	Nov. 7–Sept. 16, AD 680–681	Emperor Constantine IV	Patriarch George I of Constantinople	300	Monotheism; the human and divine wills of Jesus
Second Council of Nicaea	Sept. 24–Oct. 23, AD 787	Constantine VI and Empress Irene (as regent)	Patriarch Tarasios of Constantinople, legates of Pope Adrian I	350	Iconoclasm

APPENDIX B

Some Western Cults—Compared

Christian Beliefs	Jehovah's Witness	Christ. Sci.	Mormons	Unitarian/Universalist	Scientology	Unification	New Age
One	NO	NO	NO	NO	NO	NO	NO
Two	NO	NO	NO	NO	NO	NO	NO
Three	NO	NO	NO	NO	NO	NO	NO
Four	NO	NO	YES	NO	NO	NO	NO
Five	YES	NO	YES	NO	NO	YES	NO
Six	YES	NO	YES	NO	NO	YES	NO
Seven	NO	NO	NO	NO	NO	NO	NO
Eight	YES	YES	NO	NO	NO	NO	NO
Nine	NO	NO	YES	NO	NO	YES	NO
Ten	NO	NO	YES	NO	NO	NO	NO
Eleven	NO	NO	NO	NO	NO	NO	NO
Twelve	NO	NO	NO	NO	NO	NO	NO
Thirteen	NO	NO	YES	NO	NO	NO	NO
Fourteen	YES	YES	YES	NO	NO	YES	NO
Fifteen	NO	NO	YES	NO	NO	YES	NO

*Refer to the Introduction for a list of the beliefs.

APPENDIX C

Some of the Anachronisms and Historical Inaccuracies in the Mormon Scriptures[*]

A) In 1 Nephi 2:5–8, it is stated that the River Laman emptied into the Red Sea. There is no historical record that there has ever been a river in Arabia that emptied into the Red Sea.

B) Nephi states that only the family of Lehi, Ishmael, and Zoram were left in Jerusalem, in 600 BC, to migrate to the New World. These totaled—fifteen persons, plus three or four girls—no more than about twenty in all. Yet in less than thirty years (2 Nephi 5:28), they had multiplied such that they divided into two nations (2 Nephi 5:5–6, 21). After arriving in America in 589 BC, they built a temple like Solomon's. Yet Solomon's temple required some 153,000 workers and thirty thousand overseers (1 Kings 5:13, 15; 6:1, 38; 9:20–21; 2 Chron. 2:2, 17–18) to complete in seven and a half years. How mostly unskilled children could have duplicated the feat in the nineteen years stated is a difficult question. Nor is it clear where all the raw materials and alloys such as

---

[*] Primary source: Gleason Archer Jr., *A Survey of Old Testament Introduction*, Moody Publishers, 2007.

iron, copper, brass, silver, and gold were found in the great abundance needed. There is also a lack of any evidence of such a structure ever having been built anywhere in North America.

C) According to Alma 7:10, Jesus was born in Jerusalem, rather than the predicted (Micah 5:2) and recorded (Luke 2:4) Bethlehem.

D) Helaman 14:20 and 29 states that darkness covered the whole earth for three days at the death of Christ versus the three hours recorded in Matthew 27:45 and Mark 15:33. How would the woman and others arriving at the tomb have been able to see the stone rolled away, etc.?

E) Alma 46:15 indicates that people were called Christians in 73 BC, rather than being first called that at Antioch (Acts 11:26).

F) Helaman 12:25–25—allegedly written in 6 BC—quotes John 5:29 as a prior source, despite the fact that John's gospel was recorded some eight-plus decades later.

G) Numerous times, the Nephites are stated to have possessed the Mormon scriptures back in 600 BC, but the Mormon scriptures often quote from or allude to Bible passages written in the exilic or post-exilic period of the Old Testament. Malachi and Daniel are two such books quoted by the Book of Mormon that was supposedly existed prior to 600 BC.

H) There are also *many*—over four hundred!—copied, plagiarized, and lightly edited passages from the New Testament in the Book of Mormon, et al.

I) Perhaps the most embarrassing Smith fraud involved the Book of Abraham in *The Pearl of Great Price*. Smith's ego was apparently limitless as he proclaimed he had the gift of translating the Ancient Egyptian language. Finding what he was sure were ancient Egyptian papyri, he claimed that one of the scrolls was the Book of Abraham. Smith published the "translation," which included three drawings as well as his interpretation of the drawings. Alas, in 1967, this Smith fraud was exposed. The papyrus Smith claimed the Book of Abraham was actually translated by real Egyptian language scholars and found to be, in essence, a procedure to prepare bodies to be embalmed for burial. *Not one word* of Smith's supposed translation matches the actual translation. The illustrations actually depicted the god of embalming (Anubis) hovering above the head in the form of a bird, the canopic jars containing the man's innards set beneath his bier, and the deceased led into the presence of Osiris, the infernal deity who judged the souls of the dead. The last illustration was what Smith had identified as Abraham sitting on the Pharaoh's throne! This exposed Smith as a total fraud but, apparently, it was not a death blow to the movement.

APPENDIX D

Comparison Charts of Christianity and Islam

Jehovah God vs. Allah

The Nature of God	Christianity: Jehovah	Islam: Allah
Does God change?	God does not change. James 1:17: *Every good gift and every perfect gift is from above, and cometh down from the Father of lights, with whom is no varying, neither shadow of turning.*	Allah of Islam changes. Surah 2:106: *If We supersede any verse or cause it to be forgotten, We bring a better one or one similar. Do you not know that Allah has power over all things!*
Is God loving?	God loves everyone. John 3:16: *For God so loved the world that He gave His only begotten Son . . .*	Allah is temperamental. Surah 32:13: *If we so willed, we could have brought every soul its true guidance, but the word from me will come true: "I will fill Hell with demons and men all together."*
Is God deceptive?	God cannot lie. Titus 1:2: *In hope of eternal life, which God, that cannot lie, promised before the world began.*	Allah deceives. Surah 8:30: *They plot and plan, and Allah, too plans, but the best planners [deceivers] is Allah.*
Is God a Trinity?	God is Triune. Father is God: John 6:27 Son is God: Colossians 2:9 Spirit is God: Acts 5:3–9	Trinity is blasphemy. Surah 5:73: *They do blaspheme who say God is one of three . . . for there is no Allah except one Allah.*
Who is in the Trinity?	Father, Son, and Holy Spirit. Matthew 28:19: *Go ye therefore, and teach all nations,*	Islam believes that the Christian Trinity is God the Father, God the Mother (Mary),

	baptizing them in the name of the Father, and of the Son, and of the Holy Ghost.	**and God the Son (Jesus).** Surah 5:116: *And behold! God will say: O Jesus the son of Mary didst say unto men, "Worship me and my mother as gods" in derogation of Allah?*

Jesus of the Bible vs. Jesus of the Qur'an

The Nature of Jesus	Christianity: Yeshua	Islam: Isa
Is Jesus created?	**Jesus is not created.** Colossians 1:17: *And he is before all things, and by him all things consist.*	**Jesus was created.** Surah 3:59: *The similitude of Isa before God is as that of Adam; He created him from dust . . .*
Is Jesus Lord or an Apostle?	**Jesus is Lord.** John 14:6: *Jesus saith unto him, I am the way, the truth, and the life: no man cometh unto the Father but by me.*	**Jesus is just an Apostle.** Surah 4:171: *O people of the book, commit no excess of your religion: nor say of Allah aught but truth, Christ Isa the son of Mary was an apostle of Allah.*
Was Jesus crucified?	**Jesus was crucified.** 1 Corinthians 2:2: *For I determined not to know any thing among you, save Jesus Christ, and him crucified.*	**Jesus was not crucified.** Surah 4:157: *That they said in boars "We killed Christ Isa, the son of Mary" . . . but they killed him not, nor crucified him.*

Jesus vs. Muhammed

Jesus vs. Muhammad	Jesus	Muhammed
Son of God or just a man?	**Jesus is Son of God.** John 10:36: *Say ye of him, whom the Father hath sanctified, and sent into the world, Thou blasphemest; because I said, I am the Son of God?*	**Jesus is just a man.** Surah 18:4–5: *And it warns those who say: "Allah has taken a son." Surely, of this they have no knowledge, neither they nor their fathers; it is a monstrous word that comes from their mouths, they say nothing but a lie.*

CULTS AND CHRISTIAN COUNTERFEITS

Know the thoughts of men?	**Jesus knew the thoughts of men.** Revelation 2:23: *And all the churches small know that I am he which searcheth the reins and hearts.*	**Muhammed does not know the thoughts of men.** Surah 11:31: *I do not say to you that I possess the treasuries of Allah, and I do not know the unseen.*
Advocate with the Father?	**Jesus is our advocate.** 1 John 2:1–2: *My little children, these things I write unto you, that ye sin not. And is any man sin, we have an advocate with the Father, Jesus Christ the righteous: And he is the propitiation for our sins: and not for ours only, but also for the sins of the whole world.*	**Muhammed is not our advocate.** Surah 9:80: *(It is the same) whether or not you beg forgiveness for them. If you beg forgiveness for them seventy times Allah will not forgive them, for they have disbelieved in Allah and His Messenger. Allah does not guide the evildoers.*
Use of Sword?	**Jesus forbids the use of the sword.** Matthew 26:52: *Then said Jesus unto him, Put up again thy sword into his place: for all they that take the sword shall perish with the sword.*	**Muhammed urges the use of the sword.** Surah 8:65: *O Prophet, urge the believers to fight. If there are twenty patient men among you, you shall overcome two hundred, and if there are a hundred, they shall overcome a thousand unbelievers, for they are a nation who do not understand.*
Forgiveness or Revenge?	**Jesus teaches forgiveness.** Matthew 5:38–39: *Ye have heard that it hath been said, An eye for an eye, and a tooth for a tooth: But I say unto you, That ye resist not evil: but whosoever shall smite thee on thy right cheek, turn to him the other also.*	**Muhammed teaches revenge.** Surah 2:194: *The sacred month for the sacred month, prohibitions are (subject to) retaliation. If any one aggresses against you, so aggress against him with the likeness of that which he has aggressed against you.*
Sinless or Sinful?	**Jesus is Sinless.** 1 Pete 2:21–22: *For even hereunto were ye called: because Christ also suffered for us, leaving us an example, that ye should follow his steps: Who did no sin, neither was guile found in his mouth.*	**Muhammed is Sinful.** Surah 18:110: *Say: "I am only a human like you, revealed to me is that your God is One God. Let him who hopes for the encounter with his Lord do good work, and not associate anyone with the worship of his Lord."*

BRUCE D. WOODS

Salvation in Christianity vs. Islam

Salvation	Christianity: Grace	Islam: Straight Path
Is man born with Original Sin?	**Man is born with Original Sin.** Romans 5:12: *Wherefore, as by one man sin entered into the world, and death by sin; and so death passed upon all men, for that all have sinned.*	**Man has no original sin. Sin by deed only.** Surah 2:37: *Thereupon, Adam learned from his Lord some words and repented and his Lord accepted his repentance for He is much-relenting and most compassionate.* Surah 6:164: *Shall I seek a lord other than Allah, while He is the Lord of all things? No person earns any sin except himself only and no bearer of burdens shall bear the burden of another.*
Is Jesus the only way to salvation?	**Jesus is the only way.** Philippians 2:10–11: *That at the name of Jesus every knee should bow, of things in heaven, and things in earth, and things under the earth; And that every tongue should confess that Jesus Christ is Lord, to the glory of God the Father.*	**Jesus was a man and a worshipper of Allah.** Surah 19:30: *He (the baby) said: "I am the worshipper of Allah. Allah has given me the Book and made me a Prophet."*
Is salvation open to everyone?	**Salvation is offered to all.** Romans 10:13: *For whosoever shall call upon the name of the Lord shall be saved.*	**Salvation is only in Allah's hands.** Surah 2:284: *Allah forgives whom He pleases, and punishes whom He pleases, for Allah has power over all things.*
Grace or Works?	**Grace alone saves.** Ephesians 2:8–9: *For by grace are ye saved through faith; and that not of yourselves: it is the gift of God: Not of works, lest any man should boast.*	**Good works cancel bad deeds.** Surah 11:114: *For those things that are good remove those that are evil.*
Is there assurance in salvation?	**There is Eternal Security.** John 10:28: *And I give unto them eternal life; and they shall*	**Jihad is the only eternal security.** Surah 3:157: *And if you are slain, or*

	never perish, neither shall any man pluck them out of my hand.	*die in the way of Allah, forgiveness and mercy from Allah are far better than all they could amass.*
Is salvation coerced?	**God forces no one to salvation.** Revelation 3:20: *Behold, I stand at the door, and knock: if any man hear my voice, and open the door, I will come in to him, and will sup with him, and he with me.*	**Allah forces worship.** Surah 2:193: *Fight against them until there is no dissension, and the religion is for Allah.* Surah 9:29: *Fight those who neither believe in Allah nor the Last Day, who do not forbid what Allah and His Messenger have forbidden, and do not embrace the religion of the truth, being among those who have been given the Book, until they pay tribute out of hand and have been humiliated.*

ACKNOWLEDGMENTS

To the wonderful staff of Mountain Arbor Press, thank you for transforming my gruesome draft into a book that might prove informative to a few people. You make it almost fun!

To the many wonderful church schoolteachers, pastors, and dedicated lay people whom God allowed me to meet, learn from, and fellowship with, I thank you deeply. It's a joy to be a child of God!

BIBLIOGRAPHY

Archer, Gleason. *A Survey of Old Testament Introduction*. Chicago: Moody Bible Institute, 2007.

Brown, Harold O. J. *Heretics: Heresy and Orthodoxy in the History of the Church*. Peabody: Hendrickson Publishers, Inc., 1998.

Gonzales, Justo L. *The Story of Christianity: The Early Church to the Reformation. Volume 1.* Peabody: Prince Press, 2005.

Gonzales, Justo L. *The Story of Christianity: Vol. 2: The Reformation to the Present Day.* Peabody: Prince Press, 2005.

Guthrie, Shirley. *Christian Doctrine*. Louisville: Westminster John Knox Press, 1994.

Ligonier Ministries. *A Field Guide on False Teaching*. Orlando: Ligonier Ministries, 2020.

Martin, Walter – ed. by Ravi Zacharias, "The Kingdom of the Cults", Bethany House, revised edition 2003.

Martin, Walter. *The Kingdom of the Occult.* Edited by Jill Martin Rische and Kurt Van Gorden. Nashville: Thomas Nelson, 2008.

Shelley, Bruce. *Church History in Plain Language*. Nashville: Thomas Nelson, 2008.

Sire, James W. *Scripture Twisting: 20 Ways the Cults Misread the Bible*. Westmont: InterVarsity Press, 1980.

The Book of Concord. Translated by Theodore Tappert. Minneapolis: Fortress Press, 1959.

The Westminster Assembly. *The Westminster Confession of Faith*. 1646.

Internet Sites

(Please note that internet sites go up, go down, and often change . . .)

Apologetics Press. "Islam and Other World Religions." https://apologeticspress.org/category/islam-and-other-world-religions/

Nehls, Gerhard and Walter Eric. "Christian Controversy: A Teacher's Textbook." Nairobi: Life Challenge Africa, 2010. http://answering-islam.org/Nehls/tt2.pdf.

www.ingramcontent.com/pod-product-compliance
Lightning Source LLC
Chambersburg PA
CBHW071249070526
44583CB00017B/2394